A Beautiful Patience

A Beautiful Patience

A Memoir of Marriage, Motherhood, and a Mission to Gaza

SAMAIYA MUSHTAQ

With a Foreword by Dr. Omar Suleiman

Daybreak Press
3533 Lexington Avenue North, Arden Hills, MN 55126
www.rabata.org/daybreakpress | daybreakpress@rabata.org

ISBN (print): 978-1-967369-03-4
ISBN (ebook): 978-1-967369-04-1
LCCN: 2025946271

Cover art and design: Zainab Arshad
Typesetting: Muhammad Hozien | scholarlytype.com

Printed in the United States of America

*For Allah, for my family, and for the people of Palestine
who inspired this book*

It is not the eyes that are blind, but the hearts.
—Quran 22:46

Contents

Foreword

Some stories are powerful because they are rare. Others because they are honest. This one is both.

A Beautiful Patience is at once a story all readers will find some deep resonance and be able to identify with, but also one that will leave most of us only hoping to aspire to.

This narrative is unique in that it provides an intimate dual window into both a father's medical missions in Gaza and the parallel journey of his wife's sacrifices at home. We also get a glimpse of the incredible sacrifice and hardships borne by the people of Gaza themselves.

The work is a profound testimony of faith, sacrifice, service, hardship, loss, and love.

Since the start of the Gaza genocide, a heroic legion of Muslims and non-Muslims alike have put their very lives on the line and abandoned their cocoons of safety—the predictability of their routines and the creature comforts they are used to. Inspired by faith and the sense of duty that springs forth from the bonds of solidarity, they have decided to rush headlong into what has become quite literally an inferno of destruction and death. Like all of us, they have experienced the profound dissonance caused by sitting at home surrounded by the laughter and play of their own children while simultaneously transfixed in horror as they scroll through image after gut-wrenching image of the children of Gaza murdered or maimed, writhing in agony. Or getting ready to begin a meal at a restaurant, but then recalling the images of literal starvation and famine ravaging the Gaza Strip. Unlike most others, however, this legion of individuals from across the globe—including here in our own communities across North America—refused to let that dissonance dissipate and take a back seat to the aforementioned "cocoon." They refused the position of spectator and, instead, were spurred to action, even at great peril to themselves.

This is one such story. The story of one family's sacrifice—a husband and father assisting the injured and ill of Gaza under bombardment, and a wife and mother sharing this experience through inextricably linked sacrifices and struggles of her own thousands of miles away.

Even more importantly, this is a story that provides us yet another window into the remarkable courage and resilience that have come to define the people of Gaza. A people who have come to be characterized by a valor and generosity of spirit, even under fire and bombardment, that merit our bearing witness at the very least and, hopefully, our study and reception as a source of inspiration and instruction.

May Allah bless Dr. Samaiya and Dr. Mahmoud for sharing this story with us all and contributing to the global witnessing on behalf of Gaza that we are all experiencing unfold before our eyes. May Allah bless and reward Dr. Mahmoud and all of his colleagues both inside and outside of Gaza for risking life and limb to serve its people, as well as those who sacrificed and struggled along with them (even if separated by oceans and time zones), giving them the strength and encouragement that buoyed their service and resolve. And may Allah heal and cure and protect all of the people of Gaza, have mercy upon those who have perished, and allow us to see, very soon, the hardships and horrors of Gaza replaced with victory, a just peace, and the laughter and play of its children.

—*Dr. Omar Suleiman*

THE GAZA STRIP

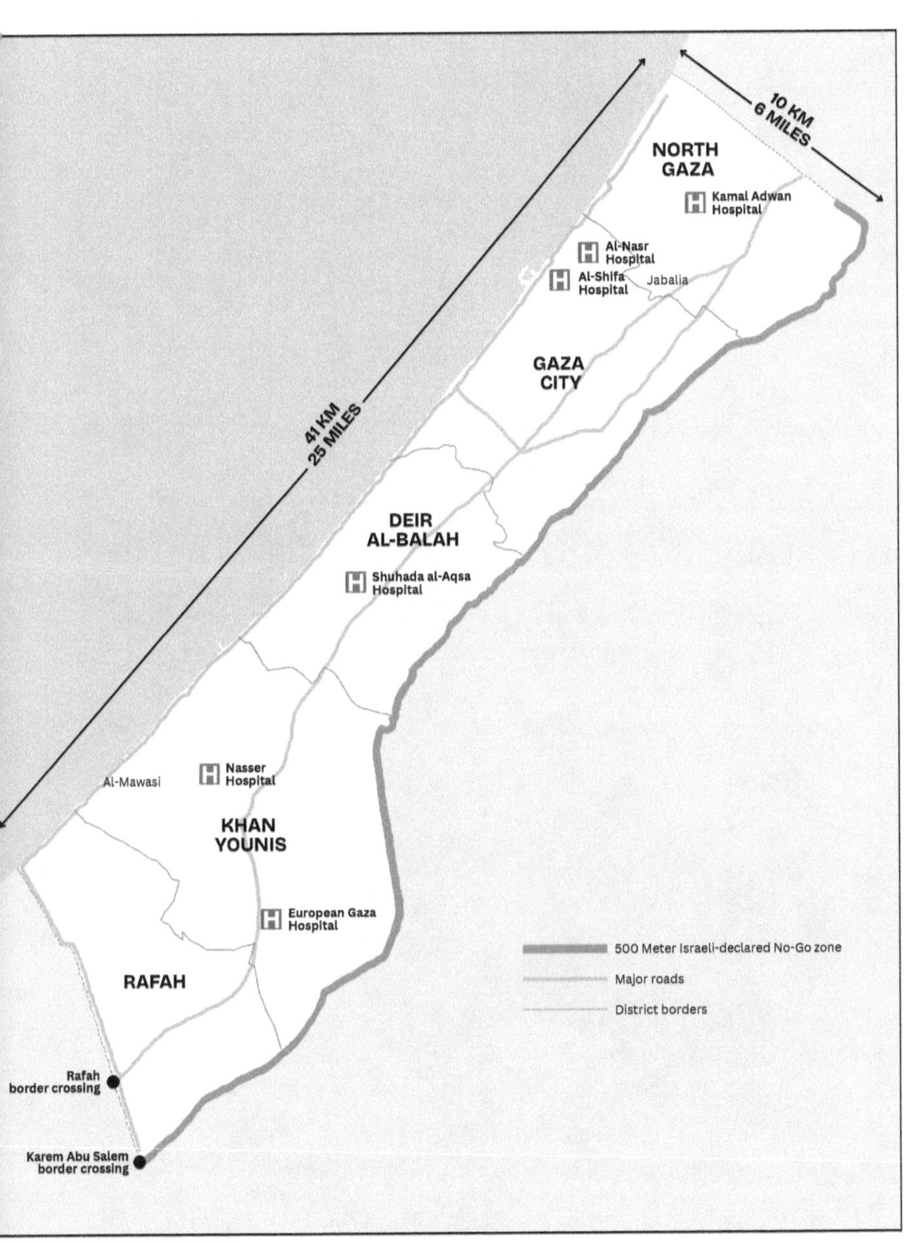

Part One

"Baba's not here," Maymuna says, lifting her head up from her crib mattress, her fine brown curls falling over her face in a messy mop.

"No. No, he's not here, mama," I say. I bend over the crib and raise her hand to kiss it. The back of her hand is pillowy soft with dimpled pits for knuckles, so unlike the rugged terrain of bone and veins jutting through mine.

"Baba *nayim*," she says, resting her head back down and snuggling closer to her stuffed flamingo. Baba's sleeping.

Perhaps he is. I imagine Mahmoud in his black zip-up hoodie, leaning forward in his seat with the hood stretched over his head, his forehead pressed against the tray table in front of him. I could never understand how he was able to nap on airplanes that way, but he would, for hours. I glance at the glowing white numbers on the base of Maymuna's sound machine. It is just two hours into his flight to Cairo, but I'm willing to bet Maymuna is right—Mahmoud is sleeping.

"Baba *nayim* on the *tiyarah*," I say, weaving in the vocabulary I've picked up from the Arabic alphabet flashcards Maymuna flips through with Mahmoud. Baba's sleeping on the plane.

"Baba's not heeeere," Maymuna says, with just a slight change in inflection. She is in the peak of her repeating phase, and this is one of her favorite refrains.

I know this circular conversation with a toddler well, and it's my cue to end the night. "I'll see you in the morning, Maymuna," I say, and she doesn't protest. "Mama loves you."

I close the door quietly behind me. As I hear Maymuna lying in the dark singing her ABCs, I imagine the sweet little toddlers in Gaza, two- and three-year-olds, all the little children I've seen through my phone screen over the last five months—children just like our daughter—who have songs inside of them but are too hungry, too tired, and in too much pain to sing. And that is why Baba isn't here.

When Mahmoud first broaches the idea of going to Gaza for a medical mission, it surprises me that I don't refuse immediately.

He feels called to go, he says. He has seen the massacres unfold the same as we all have, virtually tuning in to and away from people who have been living it daily for five months and livestreaming their deaths and destruction on Instagram. But he has something to offer. He is a wound care physician and can provide direct aid.

I understand where he is coming from. I'm a doctor too. But I had Maymuna two years ago, followed by our now four-month-old son, Qasim, and I am a mother first.

"Think about the kids," I tell Mahmoud. "What if you don't come back? They're too young to even remember you. They will only have my stories of you."

My own father's father died when my father was six. He left for Hajj, the Muslim pilgrimage, at thirty-nine—the same age Mahmoud is now. On the bus back to Mecca during the last leg

4

of the journey, he suddenly died. He was buried there just hours later in Jannat al-Mu'alla; his was one in the constant stream of Salat al-Janaza—funeral prayers—recited in al-Masjid al-Haram that year. I wonder how my grandmother even received the news in 1960s Pakistan that her husband was not returning home to her and their four children, one of whom was disabled.

Growing up, I knew almost nothing about my *dada* other than this. My father was never truly able to articulate the legacy that his father's early death left upon him. I remember once pulling out a framed photo of my grandfather that was tucked away in a drawer in my parents' dresser and setting it on top. It was the first time I remember seeing my grandfather. He was handsome and smiling, with a bright eagerness in his eyes that I didn't recognize in my father's. When I went into my parents' room to say good night to them later that evening, the picture had been put back into the drawer. My father did not say why, and I did not ask; perhaps even at seven I knew that doing so would not reveal an answer.

I worry that if Mahmoud's absence is a permanent one, there will be no one to teach Qasim how to be a father himself one day. I also count on Mahmoud for our children's religious education, given his fluency in Arabic and his memorization of the entire Quran. But the biggest fear I have is the potential for grief to mutate his legacy, and I say this to him in a fight some days later in a moment of anger that I immediately regret: "The rest of the world might lionize your altruism, but I see this as deeply selfish."

I project what my kids may think of their father if he dies— that he didn't just pass away on a religious rite, he left them to go to a war zone and was killed. He may not have sought death, but he knew that it was within reach and he chose to go anyway. I worry if that belief sinks its hooks into them, they might take

the religious values that brought Mahmoud to this decision—
those of striving and doing good and having faith in God—and
reject them completely.

I don't know fully where I stand, but I already know where
all the conversations we will have over the next two weeks will
lead. Mahmoud will go to Gaza.

It is the summer of 2017, and my intestines are writhing in pain. I
am recovering from a bout of *Campylobacter jejuni*, a gastrointestinal (GI) infection that, if my memory of medical school micro-
biology serves me, comes from undercooked chicken—likely
from the Mediterranean-buffet restaurant where I attended a
fundraising iftar. I've lost ten pounds off my already petite frame
and can hardly stand. I don't want to go to tonight's Ramadan
banquet, but I am the one who coordinated this hundred-person
iftar for the medical center, so I must.

I peel myself off the couch in my apartment, the one I moved
into after my divorce, and I get myself ready. I've delegated many
of the big things, so there is little to do once I arrive except present myself as more jovial than I feel. One of the administrative
coordinators has arranged the food, and Maheen, an acquaintance of mine who is also in residency, said she'd ask her coresident to lead Maghrib prayer.

The banquet has come together so beautifully, and we have an
excellent turnout. But now there is only one minute left until it's
time to break the fast. I ask Maheen where her colleague is—we
can't delay Maghrib, especially during Ramadan. She says he's
coming; he just isn't here yet.

A dark-haired man in a crumpled light-blue button-down and gray slacks that are just a little too short for someone so tall makes his way to Maheen, with little sense of urgency. He checks his phone for the time. I don't wait for introductions; I don't ask names. "Are you the one leading Maghrib?" I ask, trying to veil my slight annoyance at his tardiness.

"Yes, Samaiya, this is—" Maheen starts.

"Thank you, thank you so much for doing this. Please, come this way," I gesture to the front of the large white tablecloths we have laid out to cover the floor where we will pray.

Someone has jumped up to make the *adhan*, the call to prayer, and the people attending the iftar begin to reach for the dates placed in the center of each table to break their fasts. The man in the blue shirt leads the prayer, and once he concludes, I make some opening remarks for the event. It's our organization's first campus-sponsored iftar at the medical center, and I am proud to see our efforts to connect our wider Muslim community come to fruition.

I feel my guts churn. I wrap up my comments quickly and slip away to the bathroom. This is how the rest of the evening goes for me, darting in and out of the bathroom while greeting residents and medical students and their families, and even some faculty who have come to lend their support. By the end of it, after the dinner, the speakers, and the tea, I am spent, but I am still standing.

The administrative coordinator concludes the evening and thanks me for the work I've put in. The medical students and the residents start to leave, and I can't help but notice that they are mostly leaving in twos, threes, or fours—couples and young families.

I have ignored the ache in my heart for most of the month of Ramadan, a time that is usually spent with loved ones. I am alone, waking up by myself for *suhur* and eating my iftar on my own at the dining table I purchased from an amateur woodworker on Facebook Marketplace. Some nights I go to the mosque twenty minutes away, but the night prayers are so late during the summer that I am too sleep-deprived to function on service the next day. And when I return, it is to my own one-bedroom apartment—cozy, but dark and quiet.

I am twenty-five and a second-year psychiatry resident. An overachiever in school and at work, I see my personal life as a failure. I thought I would have had a child by now, or at least be planning to have one soon. Instead, here I am walking to my car by myself after hosting a community iftar—with no community of my own. I cry on the short drive to my apartment and then collapse into bed in my dress and tights, holding my cramping stomach—alone, yet thankful to be free from a much more painful loneliness.

It is the summer of 2016, and I am sitting in my parents' formal living room. I had thought this was when my husband and I would let our families know that we were ending our marriage, but instead, his parents and my own are trying to talk me out of it. I hang my head down and stare at the paisley floral swirls of the Persian rug beneath my feet, avoiding eye contact. My husband and I have been physically separated for months, but the emotional chasm between us has always been there; I was just naive enough to think that marriage would close it.

Two months before my wedding in 2013, I was sitting across from a friend at the Au Bon Pain on my medical school campus expressing my disquietude about our engagement. "It feels like I can't really reach him, like there's this missing chip, this inability to emotionally attune," I had told her.

She floated the idea of breaking off the engagement, or at least postponing the wedding. "You're so young. You have so much time."

"I don't," I lamented. "The deposit has already been paid. The invitations are out."

Soon after our wedding, I started my third year of medical school and, with it, my clinical rotations. I was young—twenty-two—and sensitive and empathetic. In addition to the long hours, I was witnessing and being shaped by all the suffering of the patients I encountered. I'd come home, desperate to process, to a husband who didn't know how to do that with me, and I started to wonder if the lack of awareness was actually a lack of interest.

The first patient I ever saw die was on trauma surgery night call. Motorcycle versus car. One minute we were rounding in the surgical ICU and everything was normal, and the next minute beeping alarms went off and the whole team descended on one patient's bed. They determined that he wasn't even stable enough to go to the operating room and attempted a rescue bedside laparotomy—cutting his belly open right there on the hospital stretcher to try and stop a bleed. They packed his open abdomen full of towels. The bleeding wouldn't stop. The resident got on top of him and started chest compressions. The intern took over. They kept switching, trying to cling on, and he kept slipping away, his life evaporating into the ether. Blood sloshed everywhere on the floor; the intern's scrub pants went from blue to maroon at the knees. Someone called time of death. It was terrible—the most gruesome thing I'd seen. I went home that night shell-shocked and found my husband watching TV, leftovers for me still warm on the stove and the dishes put away. He said hello and went back to his show. I had tried to connect enough times to know that he wouldn't understand why I was so troubled by what I'd just witnessed. I went into our room, locked the door, and crouched against the door, holding myself and bawling over the man I had seen die. My husband was supporting me in the way he knew how, but not in the way I needed.

I had thought moving back to Texas, our home state, would help bridge the distance between us, but it wasn't the panacea we had hoped. Soon after we moved, I moved in with my parents. We tried counseling. Our marriage therapist, bless his heart, floundered along with us. My development into a psychiatrist, or perhaps just more years of my life, more years of our marriage, only brought my unmet needs into sharper focus, and I developed a clearer language for what was missing between us. I desperately needed curiosity, conversation, a deeper emotional connection, and I felt angry at myself for it. Why was I so complex? Why couldn't I be happy with the needs that were met?

While my parents knew how unsettled I felt within my marriage, they encouraged me toward tolerance and gratitude. In their idea of love, transactions were currency. My husband took me traveling, he earned a decent living, and there was nothing egregious like physical abuse going on—therefore, I ought to be able to love him. My inability to do so spoke to a failure within me, not an inherent incompatibility between the two of us. In our collectivist culture, the source of my dissatisfaction appeared foolish, and my separation self-indulgent. Within that framework, it looked like my husband was steadfastly trying to make our marriage work, and I was the impudent wife reneging on a commitment, threatening my own and their standing in our Desi community, and throwing my life away—all over some self-actualized delusion that he and I didn't "connect."

But I had tried, despite my misgivings about our emotional compatibility from the beginning. I persisted. I waited to be asked about my day, for my spouse to be interested in what I was doing and how I was changing. I had waited to be known. Then I stopped waiting, and I started asking. Then I started begging. Then I began wilting, and now, here I am in my parents' living room, with the wisdom to know that I can no longer carry on living a life without the emotional intimacy I need.

It is agony witnessing the dragged-out demise of our marriage—cutting it open to dissect what has gone wrong, trying to stop the bleed, resuscitating it. Him clinging on. Me trying to let go. Somebody needs to call it. I want to melt into the hand-knotted silk of the rug, cease to exist to avoid what is coming next. I look up at my husband and see the pain in his eyes, and feeling like the worst human being on earth, the killer of our marriage, as if it were all me, as if none of it were him, I say, "I'm sorry. I can't do this anymore."

I've started my third year of psychiatry residency, and after I wrap up with my therapy patients, I make the drive up the Dallas North Tollway so I can lie on my own psychoanalyst's couch, stare at the peculiar but evocative artwork hanging above it, and untie the many threads of my early childhood and my deceased marriage. I think I want to meet someone again, but I left my marriage making peace with the idea that I might never. I live alone and without a TV; I quite like my own company now. I spend many a quiet night sitting out on my balcony now that the mosquitoes of summer have started to die off, reading a book and enjoying the muggy, almost fall breeze.

I am also reminded here and there that I'm not so marriageable the second time around, and my belief about the potential of my life is molded accordingly. These reminders show up in small slights, like when I ask a friend if she knows anyone with whom I would hit it off and she replies with, "Even my friends who haven't been married before can't find someone. I'm sorry." Or at a Desi wedding when some old friends who are single and predicting when each will get married skip right over me. My mother, likely wanting to spare me from disappointment, projects her own dwindled expectations onto everyone else: "He won't like you once he learns you're divorced," she anxiously laments about a prospective match. Her advice is to display my "scarlet letter" up front while also talking about it as little as possible, glossing over it as inconsequential.

The first man I connect with postdivorce asks me for further details of my marriage's demise. I give him a summary statement, trying to capture the nebulousness objectively, without a whole lot of finger-pointing. "That's it?" he asks me, puzzled but also seemingly disappointed at the absence of drama. He then proceeds to share that he, too, is divorced, and tells me about how he found his wife cheating on him at their five-star resort in Mexico on their honeymoon.

Then there is the old acquaintance I used to know when I was married, and with whom I had recently reconnected. We plan to meet, but he forgets because he's getting a haircut. When we do finally meet, he remarks, "I don't mind," offering an approval

I hadn't sought. "As long as you don't write a memoir or something about it," he adds.

There's a setup by an aunty with a man who is also divorced. He asks if I would sign a prenup, should things progress. It turns out he is not divorced but in the process of divorcing—in the midst of mediations around alimony and property—and I am a sounding board for his frustration with them. I turn him down and wonder if it is impractical to hope to nurture anything new where something once died.

Doris Ackers throws a tissue box at Mahmoud, and this is how we meet. She is seventy years old and entirely too demented to be living alone; she desperately needs a nursing home and has been languishing in the hospital for months waiting for one. Mahmoud is the resident on her primary team, and he has consulted the psychiatry service to help manage her agitation. I am the psychiatry resident on call.

Only this is not how we meet if you ask Mahmoud, because he remembers me from the first day of residency, two years prior. I was taking the elevator up to the epilepsy monitoring unit of the former Parkland Memorial Hospital (that has since been demolished), and he was going to the newborn nursery. He tried to make eye contact with me, but I was on my phone. He caught the name on my badge, but he didn't notice my wedding ring. He asked his coresident, Maheen—who, like me, is Desi—if she knew me. She told him she did, and, understanding the only reason a single, thirty-year-old man would be asking, she also let him know that I was married.

Doris Ackers is also not how we meet if you go by the definition of "meet," because we never actually cross paths while taking care of her. We talk on the phone once after she throws the tissue box, and I ask him to please have the nurses actually use the as-needed antipsychotic medications when she does these types of things, as I can see from the Medication Administration Record that they haven't been. He says he will try, and that is the extent of our conversation.

Thus it is that I don't recognize Mahmoud at the Ramadan iftar when he arrives just before Maghrib prayer. Maheen doesn't have time to introduce him before he goes up to lead salah, and he leaves to go to the mosque for Isha before I can circle back and tell him thank you.

It's not until months later that I actually have a conversation with him at an event for Muslim physicians to meet and discuss patient bias and discrimination. He's the only man there, and he's actually engaging in the discussion. I think to myself, *Hmm, this guy is pretty insightful.* He is piling some hummus onto his plate when I strike up a conversation with him, though it doesn't get very far before a woman arrives at the door and asks him, "Are you ready to go?" I leave sheepishly, wondering why these married Muslim men don't seem to ever wear a ring.

Even though I had gotten off the apps after yet another string of "hello" chats that went nowhere, and most of the people I met seemed to need therapy far more than I did (and yet were not making that drive up the Dallas North Tollway that I took twice a week), I decide to reactivate them because apparently hope springs eternal. And to my surprise, I see the hummus tray guy who left with the lady, who is also the blue shirt guy who led Maghrib, who is also the resident who wouldn't follow my recommendation to give the antipsychotics to the demented patient, who is also the resident who saw me in the elevator our very first day of residency.

Name: Mahmoud

Age: 33

Height (because it's a Muslim app and of course asks for height): 6'2"

"*The Office*, Jiujitsu, or Isha at the mosque," his tagline reads.

In his photo he is smiling, wearing a suit, and standing next to a Grand Rounds poster. He doesn't say much in his profile, but in the online world that is probably a good thing, so I swipe right.

It's a match; he had already swiped on me. A conversation window opens up and I ask, "Did you meet the hummus tray lady on here too!?" though I don't say, *The lady I thought was your wife.* It turns out that he, too, was set up by an aunty, and it, too, didn't work out. On our first outing, Mahmoud and I have poke bowls and talk about many things. All these years later, I remember none of them. I only remember thinking: *This is a guy who feels like home.*

Mahmoud has booked his ticket to Cairo. We've had several conversations over the last two weeks. We each have prayed *istikhara*—the prayer of seeking guidance when faced with a choice. A part of me begins to feel proud of him for his commitment, even if my support remains tempered with fear.

"If you say no, I won't go. I'll cancel the flight," Mahmoud says to me.

"Well, if everyone who has a family stayed back, who would go?" I say to him. I don't want to hold that sort of veto power. I also don't entirely believe him.

Before Mahmoud and I got married in the winter of 2019, I thought I was independent—I had been living on my own for two years, I had vacationed abroad by myself, and my career shift to management consulting took me to different cities every few months.

Mahmoud took independence to another level, though. We tied the knot late compared to our community's norms—he was thirty-four, and I was twenty-eight—and he had built a whole life already, centered around the mosque, jiujitsu, work as a hospitalist, and friends. It often felt like there wasn't much room for anything else, and many of our early fights were about how little time there was left for me, a small fissure that deepened after the birth of Maymuna two years into our marriage. Our couples therapist encouraged us to create conversation check-ins each week, to have date nights and six-second hugs in the morning: "Don't let go until you've counted to six." It helped, but much of our relationship dynamic seemed to be me accommodating Mahmoud. If we were the oak tree and the cypress that Kahlil Gibran poeticized spouses to be, close and yet not too close, I often felt like I was bending just slightly more toward him. Mahmoud is somewhat of a free spirit, and I had to learn to love him that way.

Even if I feel like I can say no to Mahmoud going to Gaza, I don't believe I should. We've been apart here and there when he has gone on a handful of guys' trips over the years and has worked in other cities—and these are trips that I've been on board with and that are entirely of the *dunya*—of this world. How then can I say no when this separation from our family is for the *akhira*—the afterlife? I will have to stand before God and answer for that "no" one Day.

"I don't know that I'd let my husband go," some of my friends say to me. I'm not sure what I should say in response. I don't know if I'm being principled or avoidant. "May he be facilitated to help," I say, not as a platitude, but as hope that his going is not in vain.

How Mahmoud will feel in Gaza, what he will see that he won't be able to unsee, and the enormity of the suffering there— these are the things I worry about. Yet there is also the Other Thing. The one I do not want to voice. The Other Thing feels trivial in comparison, and is anathema for a mother to say: I don't know how I am going to survive solo parenting our toddler and infant for thirteen days straight—if it does end up being just thirteen.

Maymuna, our first child, is born in the fall of 2021, and I go home a different person than I was when I arrived at the hospital. I am not head over heels in love with this baby, who looks alien, who is alien, who has made me alien to myself. My body is broken and my psyche is overwhelmed. Mahmoud holds Maymuna, coos at her, carries her in her car seat proudly to her first pediatrician's appointment, and I trail behind, limping with an icepack in my pants. I see them together, family. I find myself completely lost.

I don't understand why I cannot bake a loaf of banana bread and put away the laundry and keep the counters tidy as I usually do. I don't understand why my home has become exponentially more cluttered. I push myself to stand and walk and move for longer than I should to try and rectify it, and then the stitches from my three tears start to bleed. I want to cry when Maymuna wants to breastfeed after she's just breastfed twenty minutes ago, and thirty minutes before that, and I sit on a settee at the edge of our bed looking out the window, wanting desperately to be outside.

I change diaper after diaper after diaper, and then she poops out of the waistband of that one onto her back, so I change her outfit, and then she spits up on that outfit, so I change it again, and my days feel like an endless loop of Maymuna feeding and spitting up and pooping and napping. I start to put together that I can feel reasonably human if I shower, go outside, and have a nap—these are the three ingredients essential to the preservation of my sanity, but they are nearly impossible to have all together in the same day.

It's not only that all my time is gone. I am gone. My time isn't mine anymore, and I am not mine anymore. I am Maymuna's—to feed on, to sleep on, to spit up on. She needs me so completely that it engulfs me. It doesn't feel like I can have needs when Maymuna can't even hold her own head up.

My friends say that it gets better in six weeks. Some say it gets better in twelve. I am at three weeks, and I don't think I can make it to either one of those milestones, which seem eons away.

The sleep deprivation makes me dysphoric. I've struggled with this in Ramadan nights and in residency, but the newborn period is another beast—these aren't one-off nights in which I am sleeping poorly, but night after night, nearing a month now. I am so unhappy, and I feel so guilty for it. What is wrong with me? I have a desired child, a healthy child. Why can't I tolerate losing myself and simply be grateful for what I've gained?

Mahmoud picks up occasional shifts, and I watch him leave home with envy. He gets to leave, while I stay to care for Maymuna on my own. We are both doctors, but Mahmoud is free to still be a doctor, whereas I have metamorphosed into being only a parent—and the default parent at that. He entrusts Maymuna to me, but to whom can I entrust Maymuna? I, too, want to leave without worrying about Maymuna's next feed, but I am summoned by her cries so often that to sneak away for breakfast at the La Madeleine near our house, as I do one morning while Mahmoud and Maymuna lie asleep, feels like a truncated joy.

It was my body that gestated Maymuna, and then delivered her, and now is feeding her, and therein is the fundamental divide between Mahmoud and me. Mahmoud is enamored with Maymuna and loves to hold her. I am in service to her. He is free to love Maymuna on his terms, but I am needed by Maymuna on her terms entirely. I have no terms; I am erased.

The four walls of my bedroom start to cave in; it feels like I spend so much of my time here chained to this bed cluster feeding Maymuna. The one large eyebrow-arch window in our room has white plantation shutters that, closed, meld into the wall itself, leaving no exit, and when open, feel like the bars of a jail cell—a window to an outside world I am no longer a part of. I look out that window so often, thinking *I just need to be outside, I need to get out, I need to get out, I need to get out* . . . And then I start thinking *I need to jump out.*

My thoughts frighten me; I don't understand them. I am in a dark abyss that I seem to have descended into so slowly these past few weeks that I didn't notice how far down I'd gone, and once I do, I try to reach up and grab onto Mahmoud's hand, the home I knew before Maymuna. I call to him one day from the cave that is our room.

I tell him, "I'm not well. I need help." I don't want to say too much; I have been on the other side of this. I've signed the involuntary commitment papers that have held women just like me in the hospital. I don't want to alarm him, or perhaps I am more afraid that if I say the full truth, it won't matter at all. That because I'm alive and Maymuna is alive, there is no room for me to experience anything other than joy. And so I keep the next part to myself: *I want to jump out the window.*

But Mahmoud has had his own transformation, even if it appears less pronounced to me, and he, too, is overwhelmed. He, too, is balancing being a father with his old life, and he can't quite put together what is going on with me—a brewing postpartum depression. He doesn't know how to help me.

But I don't know how to help me either, and I don't want to be a burden, so I say no more, and I stop reaching out, and I wrap my arms around myself, in this pit that I worry is my new home.

I cut back at work because the childcare between two full-time physician schedules feels like an unwinnable game of Tetris—the various formations of blocks taking the shape of a paid nanny, a backup babysitter, a kind neighbor for the pesky forty-five-minute gap between me arriving home from the day shift and Mahmoud leaving for the night shift. Enough gaps, and I lose the game.

It takes me months to start to feel . . . not like myself, because I still feel like myself is gone . . . but to at least feel like I have my bearings around motherhood and myself as a mother. I think I've climbed out of that abyss, mostly; I can start to feel joy again.

Maymuna is sleeping more, and therefore I am sleeping more, which certainly helps. We take Maymuna all over—to meet her cousins in California, to see the Alhambra in Spain, even to visit al-Aqsa Mosque in Jerusalem. She is a sweet, happy baby, and I am relieved that my early challenges didn't render her otherwise.

Parenting between Mahmoud and me is sometimes like a three-legged race; we rely on each other, support each other, and sometimes we stumble and have to pick up again, get back into lockstep. Other times it feels like a solitary mud race, with our family sometimes resembling a scalene triangle, with Mahmoud and Maymuna much closer than I am to either of them.

I don't necessarily feel ready emotionally to have another child, but I want to give Maymuna a sibling, so in the spring of 2022, when Maymuna is eighteen months old, I get pregnant again—this time with a boy, whom we decide to name Qasim.

My second pregnancy ends up pushing me to my limits—I have hyperemesis gravidarum and can barely care for Maymuna on my own. I look and feel like death. I lose weight. The nausea and vomiting have also dried up what little was left of my supply of breast milk. Maymuna is weaned, and she and Mahmoud form an essential dyad. She is not so dependent on me; she can't be. Mahmoud, meanwhile, is more prepared, bringing me Zofran and Phenergan and sips of water, reassuring me that it will all be worth it—and also occasionally reassuring himself under the strain of this very demanding pregnancy.

As my hyperemesis improves and we ready ourselves for Qasim's arrival, I start applying for jobs. I have continued part-time in the hospital since Maymuna was born, but two years into being a mother, if I am being honest with myself, the part-time experiment hasn't worked out so well for me. I feel uneasy being financially reliant on someone, the domestic load is inequitable, and my career is stalling. And somewhere I am still the over-achiever I was before I became a mother, measuring my value in my productivity.

Days before Qasim is born, I receive a job offer in health-care administration, a pivot I'd been hoping to make for the past two years. I go to an open house where the real estate agent jokes that she hopes I don't go into labor in the living room. Days after Qasim is born, we go under contract on it—a roomier house to accommodate our growing family. It feels like my son came with his own *rizq*—his provision.

I feel a new sense of responsibility to think ahead for my now two children. I tell Mahmoud we have to get our estate in order. We aren't new parents anymore; we have a family now, and we must be caretakers of our children's *rizq*. They are an *amana*, a trust and a responsibility, and part of that is creating a plan for how they will manage financially if something happens to either or both of us.

Qasim's birth comes with all this change, and I find myself half waiting for the darkness to descend upon me the way it did after Maymuna's birth. But despite the sleep deprivation and the breastfeeding, the move to the new house and my job's impending start date, the darkness doesn't come. Perhaps because this is just how postpartum depression works, rearing its ugly head after one child and not the other. Or perhaps because the massive existential shift to matrescence already happened after Maymuna, and she paved the way for me to enjoy Qasim so much more. Perhaps I have accepted that my time and my life are not entirely mine to control, yet nor are they entirely my children's to control, and so the power struggle that existed between me and Maymuna in those early months doesn't occur between me and Qasim. Whatever the reason, the addition of Qasim to my life pulls me back from my drift, morphing our oddly shaped triangular family into a perfect square. All the change following his birth doesn't feel quite as chaotic this time, but rather like the neat unfolding of an orderly, divinely laid plan.

The days leading up to Mahmoud leaving for Gaza feel like the slow ascent to the top of a rollercoaster. My stomach churns with anxiety, so I try not to think about it too much or envision too far ahead. For now, we have today.

I've always been terrible about taking photos; Mahmoud is much better at documenting the present. I take a leaf out of his book and snap candid photos of him with Maymuna playing in the water table on our side patio, of Maymuna seated on his right leg and Qasim on his left, of him in his UC Irvine hoodie. He is smiling, but there is a sadness in his eyes. "Are you taking pictures because you think I will die there?" he asks me.

Yes, I want to say. *Yes, I am.*

Of course I don't know if Mahmoud will survive or not. We only know two doctors who have gone to Gaza, as the medical missions have only just started. Both have come back safely. But we also know that the Israeli army has never—in the three-quarters of a century since their illegal occupation of Palestine began—shied away from killing volunteers in Gaza and the West Bank. And does anyone go to an active war zone, even as a humanitarian, thinking it's not a possibility that they themselves could be one of the thousands of casualties?

I can't plan for Mahmoud to return. And it dawns on me that perhaps all these things—a second child, my new job, buying our family house, establishing our estate plan, all the steps we've taken that have made us the family I had conceived us to be from the beginning—were to create a stable enough foundation for me to continue on my own, to provide for my children and keep a roof over their heads as a single mother. I wonder if Allah is telling me, "You will be OK. You know how to be on your own."

I am anxious, certainly, but what helps me make my peace is what Mahmoud often says: *Qaddara Allahu wa ma sha'a fa'al,* Allah has decreed it, and what He wills, He does. It has been destined for him to go, and if he dies there, that was destined for him too.

And isn't that where we are all headed anyway? Certainly, the circumstances of Mahmoud's death, should it happen there, would be more violent. But perhaps part of Allah's plan, years and years ago, was to accord an understanding of how danger can find one anywhere—even within one's home—so we learn to be more ready for it when it comes.

It is the summer of 2007, and I'm about to start my senior year of high school. I take a break from sewing the COPPELL COWBOYS letters onto the pants of my senior overalls. The wealthier seniors outsource this to local moms in the neighborhood, the artsy-craftsy ones who also make mums for homecoming. I'm at the edge of the district lines, not just in neighborhood, but in socioeconomic status. I am cutting out the letters from my old T-shirts and stitching them by hand onto a hand-me-down pair of Dickies overalls.

I go downstairs and start flipping through the channels on the TV in my parents' bedroom. A documentary about Hiroshima and Nagasaki is on: *White Light/Black Rain.* I had seen the trailer a couple of days ago and was looking forward to watching it. While I'm by no means a history buff, I find the story of the atomic bomb catastrophe fascinating. I remember reading a book that described the human ash vaporized onto the walls people were walking near just before they were incinerated, a shadow of their obliteration. It disturbs me that the US did that a mere sixty years ago. It disturbs me to know what human beings are capable of doing to one another.

I'm interrupted by the doorbell. Despite it being a sunny day, I can't make out who's there through the patterned glass. I open the door a crack. It's a man in an orange checkered button-down whom I don't recognize. "Is Jackson here?" he asks.

"Uh . . . no," I say. Does he mean Thomas, next door?

Before I can ask, there is a tightening in my stomach, a knot, a strange feeling, maybe the feeling the human whose shadow was etched in stone had in the moments before the bomb fell.

My sister is at the top of the stairs coming down. It's the wrong house, I think, so I begin to close the door. That's why I want to close the door, because the man shouldn't be here.

He flings it open before I can close it.

I don't know how I end up pressed against the wall by the front door—is it the second man who comes in, or the third? Is it the first man who chases after my sister, or the fourth? I try to take my Razr phone from my back pocket, thinking I can somehow, under the watchful eyes of these five men who have stormed our home, call 911. I can somehow rescue us.

I can't. The man who has his beefy hand cupped over my mouth to keep me from screaming uses his other hand to grab my phone. He pushes me forward up the stairs; my sister is already being pushed along past the upstairs hallway, to the farthest corner of the house—my bedroom.

I am sixteen years old, yet I sleep in the same bed that my parents bought for my older two sisters when they were little, with the same heart-print canopy and duvet. I wonder if they are depraved enough to rape me in a child's bed.

They keep us moving toward my bedroom closet. I see my overalls on the ground, my fabric shears on them. Can I reach for them? I wonder. No, that's stupid. But I hope they don't see them. Because then . . . is that what they will use to kill me? Of course not, I tell myself. They must have a gun.

Two of the men begin ripping the cords off the electronics they find in my room—the purple Nickelodeon clock on my windowsill facing the backyard and my hair straightener that is sitting on the adjoining bathroom's counter. They rip them right off and then use them to bind our hands and feet. Once we are tied up on the floor of my closet, they start to ask where the valuables are. They warn us not to lie to them, claiming they know we must have some. I tell them I don't know, and they go back to ransacking my room. I watch them through the crack in the closet door. I can see them open the desk drawer where I used to keep the cash I earned from tutoring last summer—the cash I had just deposited into my very first bank account two days before.

I pray for Allah to have mercy on me. *Allah mian, rehem khao,* I beg in Urdu. I ask for forgiveness for all my mistakes. *Allah mian, maaf karo.* Then I bargain. I tell Allah all the things I'll stop doing if He lets me live. I haven't even finished my overalls, let alone had a chance to wear them. I am slated to graduate valedictorian. I'm supposed to go to college. I'm too young to die. Don't let me die, Allah!

Then I wonder how long it'll take to be found here in my closet, dead. I can't remember where our middle sister is—I think she went out with some friends. My dad is at work and he won't be back till nighttime. My mother—she'll be the one who comes home first. She went to get some groceries, and by now it must be 4:00 p.m. How much time has passed? How long have they been here, overturning mattresses, sifting through drawers? Fifteen minutes, or maybe an hour? My mother must be coming home soon, but why would she come upstairs to this remote corner? And if she does—oh no—how devastated she will be to lose two of her three kids in the same day.

But then I think, what if she comes home and interrupts the robbery? The men won't be happy. My mother will be over-come by anxiety; she might act rashly and make their job harder, and they will hurt her for it. *Mom*, I think, hoping somehow a tether remains between me and my mother, some remnant of the umbilical cord cut sixteen years ago. *Make the extra stop at Tom Thumb. Linger in the dairy aisle. Whatever you do, Mom, do not—DO NOT—come home.*

At some point life becomes less about time stamps, like the age you were when something happened or what year it was in, and the events themselves become demarcations of life. Before Maymuna. After Qasim. Before the divorce. After medical school. The deepest split in the timeline of life for me is the home inva-sion. For Mahmoud, it is 9/11.

He is in his junior year of high school when the September 11 attacks happen. The towers fall, and everything changes. His mother, like my own, wears hijab, and suddenly, even in liberal Southern California miles away from my conservative North Texas suburb, that means stares and slurs and the fear of violent retaliation for her, just as it does for my mother.

Islam is put on the map in a way that no American Muslim his age has ever seen—unwanted notoriety, scrutiny of faith practices, no-fly lists, deportations, charities shut down, FBI informants planted in mosques. A few months before Mahmoud graduates from high school, the US invades Iraq. Mahmoud stops standing up for the Pledge of Allegiance in Mr. Armstrong's AP World History class. Mr. Armstrong eventually addresses the class, saying that while he can understand the anger around the war, it would still be patriotic to stand up for the flag. Mahmoud knows he's talking to him, and he continues to stay firmly planted in his chair.

At eighteen, Mahmoud's friends are starting to ask if he'll join them at a party they're going to where they'll be drinking. He's not. He's going to the mosque and growing a beard, and in American eyes that makes him a fundamentalist, even if in his own eyes he is simply a young Muslim man coming of age.

Mahmoud graduates from high school in 2003, and a bleak summer follows. With the end of high school comes the end of playing sports, of seeing friends daily. He enrolls in community college, though with no real idea of what he's working toward. His plan of joining the military as an Arabic translator is killed along with the masses of Iraqi civilians he sees on the news, which runs nonstop in his family's living room.

One evening at the Islamic Institute of Orange County, a large mosque in Anaheim not too far from Mahmoud's home, he meets

Adam. He takes an instant liking to him. Adam is witty, and worldly, and unapologetically Muslim. After connecting a few more times at the mosque, Adam asks Mahmoud the timeless question that cements a friendship between two young men: "Do you want to join our football team?"

To a lonely Mahmoud, this is a connection he jumps at, as if catching a Hail Mary pass. "Of course I do." Adam tells Mahmoud he'll give him more details soon. There are a few guys on the team, but they're still looking for enough people to play.

Some weeks go by, and then at the mosque one day, Adam says to Mahmoud, "Listen man, I have to come clean." Mahmoud is immediately curious about what his new friend intends to reveal, and concerned by the seriousness of his expression. "There's some controversy around our team," Adam starts. "And it's part of the reason we haven't found enough guys to play. It's our name. We're Team Intifada."

Mahmoud is immediately drawn in. The Palestinians had suffered decades of abuse, and they were taking a stand, even if all they had were rocks. The Second Intifada (uprising) had been ongoing in Palestine for the last few years—epitomized by the image of Faris Odeh, the fourteen-year-old boy who stood in front of an Israeli tank throwing rocks at it and was killed with a bullet to the neck.

Adam is telling Mahmoud about the team name as if he is giving him an out, permission to change his mind. Some people have already quit at their parents' behest, he says, while others are doubling down around keeping the moniker as an ode to their Palestinian brethren.

"Are you kidding?" Mahmoud says. "I want to be on the team even more now."

Adam tells Mahmoud that there are murmurs of protestors descending upon the tournament. It may even get media attention. *Of course,* Mahmoud thinks. *They want to intimidate us. I won't be intimidated.*

He thinks about how worked up people get about a name, particularly when it is one they have trouble pronouncing. How desperately some people want to demonize the language of Muslims, how they weaponize words like jihad and shariah and intifada. And how important it is to not let them—a lesson Mahmoud's mother imparted to him when he was little.

"What's your name?" an eight-year-old Mahmoud asks the young kid sitting next to him on the bench outside their elementary school as they wait for the doors to be unlocked. They are the first ones there, Mahmoud having been dropped off by his mother on the way to her job as an English-as-a-Second-Language professor at the local community college.

"John," he replies. Mahmoud finds it curious—such an American name on someone who is distinctly Asian. The Korean kids in his school have these names: John, Kevin, and Tim. Letters that, stitched together, appear just as foreign to an Arab as the name Mahmoud does to Americans. The doors open and John takes off down the hall while Mahmoud makes his way to the basketball courts for practice.

Their coach asks everyone to introduce themselves. He lands on Mahmoud, and before he can think too much about it, before eight-year-old Mahmoud realizes that it is really about wanting things to be easier, not wanting to have to explain things so much, not wanting to ask people to pronounce a letter that doesn't even exist in their language and watch them decide the fault is with the letter, he blurts out, "I'm John."

Practice goes by, with John dribbling, passing, shooting. His coach greets his mother as she arrives to pick him up, telling her how John did great, how he's a welcome addition to the team.

Mahmoud's mother is too horrified to interrupt and correct the coach, and Mahmoud is too ashamed to meet her eyes. He sits in the backseat of the family's Ford Aerostar, keeping his head down. They pass the YMCA and the Buena Park Library before Mahmoud's mom finally breaks the silence.

"Do you know what your name means, Mahmoud?" she asks.

He knows the story of his name—of how his deceased grandmother had come in a dream to his father the very night before his mother went into labor, telling her son to name the baby Mahmoud. His mother was having twins, and Mahmoud arrived first, with Hamza following shortly after.

"That's not the only reason we named you Mahmoud," his mother says. "It's also the meaning. Your name is very special."

She tells him about the *Maqam Mahmoud*—the Praiseworthy Station of the beloved Prophet Muhammad ﷺ.* The esteemed status he holds. She gave him this name as an ode to that status. Mahmoud's heart swells with pride, overpowering the shame he had felt for trying to eschew his name in the first place.

Mahmoud's mother doesn't tell Mahmoud to stop calling himself John at basketball practice. She doesn't have to. From that day forward, there's no John, and not even any Macs or Mos—not

---

* This symbol ﷺ reads *ṣallā Allāhu 'alayhi wa sallam*, which is a phrase used by Muslims after mentioning the Prophet's name as a way of showing respect. It means "peace and blessings be upon him [the Prophet Muhammad]."

by Mahmoud's doing anyway. From that day, Mahmoud never introduces himself as anything other than Mahmoud—and he always pronounces the ح.

It takes some time to get our house back in order—mattresses have been turned over, every drawer yanked violently out of its frame, years and years of papers and mail and fragrance samples and hair ties and outgrown clothes strewn throughout. It takes some time to inventory everything that has been lost.

After this shattering experience, I am not put back together the same way. I don't die, certainly, so I am OK. I am intact. I exist. "Thank God they didn't hurt her," my mother says to her acquaintances when they call to inquire about what happened. Yet I know I am changed, because when she asks me to take out the trash at night and I have to walk into the alley, I am trembling and the handles of the trash bags become damp in my sweating hands. My heart begins to race and I am hyperventilating. I sprint to the garbage can and back as fast as I can, then immediately burst into tears and beg her please, please don't make me do that again. We don't talk about why I have stopped sleeping in my own room, where I was tied up for over an hour until we heard silence and I managed to get free of the wires on my wrist, unbind my sister's hands, and make a run for the neighbors' house. Why I instead camp out on the floor in the open loft. Or why, the first night I am home alone, I sit on the midlanding of the stairs the whole time, where I can see all the doors and windows and not miss a single sound.

My mother's loss is so much more tangible than my own. All her heirloom jewelry is gone—everything her deceased parents ever gave her. It devastates her, and she gives me a litany to recite after every salah for the next forty days. It is meant to be hopeful—if I recite it, she says, the jewelry will come back—but it feels like a penance. I will have my period in the next few weeks and will have to stop praying. Will that count against the forty consecutive days, I wonder. I am consumed with guilt because I can't help but wonder if my mother blames me for opening the door and letting the robbers in, and therefore for the loss of the jewelry. And then I worry she will blame me for the fact that my prayers weren't good enough for it all to return.

Forty days pass, and the jewelry doesn't come back. Stains from the fingerprint dust linger on the dresser drawers and the carpet in my room. The detective has shown me six driver's license photos and asked me if any one of them was among the men who invaded my home, and she says, "You must be 100% sure." But I don't know that I've been 100% sure of anything in my life, and I tell her I can't be that certain. Since there have been no other leads, they will be closing the case.

I have survived, and I am grateful. But I can't tell if I am hardened or softened. I am not so sure anymore of people's intrinsic goodness. I am not so sure of the safety of home. I'm not so sure of seeing tomorrow. I only know that at the precipice of life, at the prospect of death there in my closet, I knew only God. And it is indeed true what the poet Labid once said: "Everything other than Allah is *batil*."

"Mowing the grass." It's the Israeli strategy of periodically attacking Gaza to keep the Palestinians in check and maintain the occupation. Israel again raids the Gaza Strip in November 2008, this time in Deir al-Balah. Air strikes follow, then a ground invasion. Over a thousand Palestinians are killed. In January 2009, a British politician by the name of George Galloway forms an organization, Viva Palestina, with the goal of bypassing the years-long blockade and launching a flotilla to get crucial humanitarian aid to Gaza.

Mahmoud is working as a lab technician in Irvine, not far from the football field where he played on Team Intifada. He's still connected to the Muslim Student Union at UC Irvine, from where he has since graduated, occasionally joining some of their community events. He's applying to medical school for the second time, but with some ambivalence; not having gotten in the first time afforded him the chance to finish his *hifdh*, his memorization of the Quran, and he's in his *muraja'ah*, or review, now. The break also affords Mahmoud another opportunity—one that he sees as once in a lifetime.

Mahmoud gets the chance to join George Galloway's second convoy to Gaza as part of a US delegation of young activists. Some friends from football, including Mohamad Abdelfattah, who would eventually go to medical school with Mahmoud, are already slated to go. So is a young man from Chicago whom Mahmoud has not yet met, Thaer Ahmad. The group will spend some of their time in Egypt, but the cornerstone will be three nights in Gaza.

"Absolutely not," Mahmoud's mother says.

"You could die, baba," Mahmoud's father says. "Or, you could come back, and they will say you are Hamas."

Mahmoud is twenty-four, old enough to believe his parents are completely wrong, but not old enough to know that they are usually right; he thinks they are blowing things out of proportion. He's not going to miss out on this mission. Mahmoud doesn't know what to expect nor how he will serve the people of Gaza. All that is on his mind is being there among them.

At a meeting at the Islamic Center of Irvine the group going is briefed and told food may be limited there and to "be prepared to see the worst." It wasn't until years later that the Israeli document that calculated the number of calories necessary for Palestinians to starve but not die of malnutrition was leaked. The very document that the Israeli government used to set the upper limit of how much food they would allow into Gaza.

The flight is a long one, so Mahmoud nods off. At one point, a guy asks him in bewilderment how he manages to sleep sitting up like that. Mahmoud shrugs. "I don't know. I just sit there and think of nothing." The guy tries it, and it works.

On arriving in Egypt, Mahmoud is awestruck by the minarets. Mosques everywhere. Reminders of Allah everywhere. Some of the Muslims, however, leave more to be desired. The group ends up being in Egypt longer than planned; Israel is not allowing them to enter Gaza. Three nights become two, and Mahmoud starts to worry they won't get into Gaza at all.

During a meeting for the leadership to address the delay, George Galloway gets up to speak and gestures dramatically to the back of the room, points his finger, and declares, "Over there you see a spy from the Egyptian government." An overweight Egyptian man sitting in the back of the room with a small notebook looks up to see a hundred heads turn to him in silence. He closes his notebook, gets up, and, holding both hands up without saying a word, slowly walks backward out of the room.

This is what Muslims have done to each other, Mahmoud thinks with frustration. They cut each other at the knees, leaving the *ummah* in utter disunity. At a micro level, it is the feeling that he is getting hustled everywhere he goes—locals demanding payment for a cup of water or even directions. At a societal level, it is the betrayal and subterfuge by Arab governments that have exacerbated the Palestinians' plight.

Two nights become one, but they are ultimately allowed in. The journey from Egypt to Gaza is painfully long—an hours-long bus ride, with fat sand flies that bite buzzing in and out of the open bus windows, through which Mahmoud can see the Suez Canal.

When they enter Gaza, the transition is jarring. Everything has been brown, until they are greeted by an oasis of palm trees upon crossing through Rafah. It is a beautiful sight by itself, but it is the people who warm their hearts. Children in uniform are playing drums to greet them. People are waving Palestinian flags and signs, welcoming them with smiles and hugs. Someone hands Mohamad a bottle of water. He is conditioned to ask how much it is. The Gazan looks at him quizzically. "It's yours. *Ahlan wa sahlan.*"

They spend the next day touring Gaza, seeing the destruction from the siege. They visit the Ministry of Detainees and Ex-Detainees Affairs, where they hear from the families of loved ones who have been held hostage in Israeli prisons for years. An orphan girl shares the story of her whole family being killed in an air strike, yet she says with such conviction, "*Hasbi Allahu wa ni'mal wakil.*" Sufficient for me is Allah, and He is the best Disposer of Affairs.

They visit al-Shifa Hospital, and they hear from one of the doctors that there are no cardiac surgeons in Gaza. Mohamad shakes his head. He looks over at Mahmoud and whispers, "Bro, we gotta come back here as surgeons one day."

On the way back out of Gaza after their twenty-four hours are up, they drive along the coastline, catching a beautiful sunset. "We were treated like heroes," Mahmoud says, looking back at that first trip to Gaza. "I was so honored to be there. So blessed." He heeds Mohamad's words and reaffirms his intention to attend medical school and one day return as a doctor.

The year after the home invasion, and the year before Mahmoud goes to Gaza with the Viva Palestina convoy—and almost a decade before we meet—I move into the college dorms at Southern Methodist University. I join the Muslim Student Association, and it breathes new life into what has been my waning spirituality.

I had grown up with the rituals—the five daily prayers, the monthly fasting, the *duas* (supplications) that one recites from a book—essential worship, though the kind that can easily become a bargaining tool in front of God. "I was told that if I prayed to You with this invocation X, then You will grant me Y." The problem with this thinking is how easily it can become corrupted, and how much it can make worship lose its relevance: What's in it for me?

Sometime in college, I stumble upon the book *Purification of the Heart*, a translation and commentary on the nineteenth-century scholar Imam Mawlud's poem *Matharat al-qulub*, and it upends all of what I thought I knew, enriching the worship I had learned as a child with meaning I had not yet known.

I wasn't praying for *something*. I was praying to *someone*. The One who needs no prayer at all, but the One Whom I need for my sake. I wasn't fasting to learn what it's like to be poor and hungry, the usual reasons listed off in Sunday school. I was fasting to be reminded of my complete dependence on Him.

Since the home invasion, I had begun to take issue with the idea that some people "deserved" some things, or that being a good Muslim meant no harm would befall you, because who decides who is deserving and who isn't? I didn't "deserve" to survive the robbery because I was ranked first in my class or because it would have been hard on my mother if I had been killed. The idea that because I went through this, I deserve that, or because I had bad luck the first time, I deserve good luck the second time—this line of thinking takes Allah's mercy out of the equation. It strips the blessings we receive from Him and attributes them to us—and not even to our own inventiveness, but to our essence. It decreases our gratitude to receive something when we feel entitled to it.

I find in my faith missing pieces that I use to put myself together after the trauma of the past year. These pieces will keep me together after I move away to Nashville for medical school and after my marriage ends in divorce. *Yaqeen*, *tawakkul*, and *sabr*—conviction in Allah, reliance upon Allah, and patience from Allah—are balms for my soul, and they are what get me through Mahmoud's time in Gaza.

It is summer 2012, and Mahmoud is on a burn rotation back home in Southern California after spending two years away in

Grenada for medical school. He is joining his old friends from IIOC for a morning hike along Laguna Beach, between the ocean and some cliffs. Mahmoud, in keeping with his habit, arrives late.

It's a peaceful morning, and while Mahmoud had met another great group of Muslim guys in medical school, and Mohamad Abdelfattah had been in Grenada with him, it still feels nice to be back among his hometown friends. It is Mahmoud, Adam, Aatif, and four other guys.

As they approach the end of the hike, Mahmoud starts to see the tide get higher. It's a sudden shift. Unbeknownst to him, a riptide has developed, and the waves begin surging between the bluffs they are trekking along, becoming uncomfortably larger and louder. Aatif recognizes that these are sneaker waves—dangerous and deadly—and he hurriedly tries to reach the end of the trail. He climbs onto a large rock, and, without warning, an enormous wave batters them. When the water recedes, Mahmoud sees Aatif dangling off the bluff. Before he can find his footing again, another wave surges, and this one knocks him clean off the boulder. Aatif is submerged, out of sight.

Where the hell is he? is Mahmoud's first thought as he scans the water. Aatif's head bobs up between some boulders, his eyes glazed.

It's my fault. is Mahmoud's second thought. He was late and slowed the group down. He sees Adam on the opposite side looking for Aatif too, but he doesn't know if Adam has spotted him. These are split-second decisions—if you think too hard or waffle for too long, the consequences can be life-changing. Or life ending.

Mahmoud jumps.

He makes his way through the water while the tide is still receding and reaches Aatif, bear-hugging him from the back. He doesn't have a plan, but he thinks he can at least reorient Aatif and maybe get him to climb back up the bluffs before the next wave comes.

He is not successful. A large wave splits them apart, and Mahmoud realizes that there is a cove underneath the rocks they were hiking on. The force of the wave sucks him in, pushing him farther and farther into the cove—he doesn't know how far in it goes, so he holds his breath. What he does know is that the cove is not that high, because as the force of the wave jostles him up and down, he hits his head against the top of the arched rock.

Mahmoud loses spatial awareness, and his mind drifts to a story of some mujahideen who had to swim underwater to attack a fortress, and several of them died. He doesn't think he will die, but it crosses his mind that it's certainly possible. He tells himself to stay calm. The water recedes and finally drags Mahmoud out of the cove with it.

He catches sight of Aatif again, who looks more disoriented. Before he can move toward him, Mahmoud is sucked back into the cove. But this time he knows what to do; he goes along with the water, he doesn't fight it, and when it recedes again, he moves quickly. He finds Aatif, gets him to a rock, and they both climb up. Adam is waiting at the top to reach out and help them back onto their feet.

Once out of the water, they find a staircase that leads them to safety—into someone's backyard, where two cops in shorts pull their guns on the young men. Adam explains to the officers what happened, and the policemen put their guns away and call an ambulance. Aatif, bruised, bloodied, and battered, is transported in the back of the ambulance, while Mahmoud, relatively uninjured, rides in the front. Adam follows to the emergency room. Aatif is fortunately stable, and Adam insists Mahmoud should get checked out too—he can see several cuts on his face. Mahmoud doesn't know yet how many are on his back. Mahmoud—still a poor medical student—looks at Adam and says, "You think I want to get billed for this?"

A few days before Mahmoud leaves for Gaza, we visit his friend Abdullah Fateh. He and Mahmoud met on Hajj back in 2006, before either of them were physicians. The shaykh Mahmoud was doing his *hifdh* with was the teacher of the shaykh who was Abdullah's teacher. And Hajj buddies are for life. Abdullah had gone to Gaza for a medical mission the previous month, and was planning to go again with the same group as Mahmoud. He had obtained expiring wound care supplies from a local warehouse, and we go to Abdullah's home to collect them.

I meet Abdullah and his wife Sakeena for the first time. I ask her how she is faring. She tells me she is happy for her husband. It is striking to me that it's not even that she is reluctantly at peace with him going—she wants him to go. She asks me how it has been for me.

I think about it for a minute and then tell her, "If all I am being asked to do is care for my own two kids by myself for thirteen days, it is the very least I can do for the people of Palestine." And I mean it. My efforts feel like such a minor contribution.

While Mahmoud is putting the supplies in the car, I ask Abdullah, "You'll be with him the whole time, right?" At least

I can be assured that he'll be with a friend, whatever sense of safety that provides.

"Well," he pauses, "maybe not. I am trying to go to the north."

If I have adapted to the fear of Mahmoud going to Gaza, I feel fear upon fear for the safety of Abdullah in the north of Gaza. The north has been decimated. There is an ongoing famine. It is further blockaded within the blockade of Gaza through the Netzarim corridor—a track that the Israelis have carved through the entire width of the Gaza Strip that divides the north from the south and is named after a former settlement. The Gazans in the north are sniped holding white flags, children shot in their parents' arms. I look at Sakeena, and I don't have to say anything at all. "I support him," she says without skipping a beat. "I think he is very brave."

I don't know if Mahmoud already knows, but I don't want him to come back inside and find out. I'm silent on the drive home.

"Mahmoud, you are going to stay with the mission the whole time, right?" I ask.

"Of course," he says.

"To European Hospital, and back—nowhere else?" I ask.

He reassures me. "Yeah, we're going to be at European Hospital, honey. Nowhere else."

Part Two

Day 1: Saturday, March 23

On the way to the airport, Mahmoud makes *dua*: "*Allahumma anta al-Sahib fi al-safar wa al-Khalifah fi al-ahl.*" Oh Allah, You are the Companion of the traveler and the Guardian of the family.

We've stuffed the car with luggage filled with medical supplies, and when we get to the airport, Mahmoud stacks them all up on one of the metal carts outside. I take a photo of him in his zip-up hoodie with his stockpile. "Smile," I say, and he does—a small smile, but it's there. I don't know if it's the last photo I'll take of him, and I want to remember him happy.

He opens the two back doors of my car and ducks his head inside to kiss first Maymuna and then Qasim. I hug him tight. "I love you," I say. "I love you, too," he replies. "Come back," I tell him, as if it's a choice for either of us.

I think of the parting of Ibrahim (Abraham) (*alayhi al-salam*) from Hajar and Ismail (Ishmael) (*alayhi al-salam*) in the desert. Who is sacrificing, and who is being sacrificed? Or is it one and the same?

I had wondered in the weeks leading up to Mahmoud leaving if it was right for people with small children to put their lives at risk, or whether an exception was to be made in these circumstances—particularly in the individualistic society we live in. I sought counsel from Mahmoud's best friend, with whom he had done his *hifdh* and who had since gone on to become a shaykh. He said he believed it to be a judgment call, but a virtuous pursuit, and he said something else that surprised me: "You are a doctor as well. I have no doubt that if the children weren't here, you'd be on that plane too, serving and sacrificing alongside. But your acceptance of motherhood has certainly taken priority over that."

If it were not for Maymuna and Qasim, would I indeed be on that plane with Mahmoud? It feels hard to imagine myself right now without my children. Who would I be? What would I be living for? What would be most important to me? Those questions have entirely different answers now because of them.

If it were not for them, I would have no reason to stay behind and every reason to go with Mahmoud. Yet my children have taught me sacrifice and service better than anyone. They have pruned me of my selfishness; perhaps without them, I would not be the person I would need to be to get on that plane. The language of parenthood is universal; as James Baldwin put it, "The children are always ours, every single one of them, all over the globe." It is the children of Gaza who are also mine, who are all of ours, and it is because of them that I can see for myself the morally correct choice.

Day 2: Sunday, March 24

The day after Mahmoud leaves, I am changing Qasim's diaper when my phone starts buzzing. It's a text about a *janaza*; a friend's mother has died, and the funeral prayer is at the mosque near our home in just a few hours.

I arrive at the mosque in a hurry, my *jilbab* wrinkled and my hijab askew. The prayer hasn't started yet, and I am scanning the mosque looking for my friend. I catch her right in the middle of the front row, several women around her, consoling her. She is utterly grief-stricken.

I give her a big hug. "Please," she pleads to no one in particular, to everyone around her, her eyes glassy, unfocused. "Pray for my mother."

I imagine myself in my friend's shoes. Or socks, I suppose, since we don't wear shoes inside the mosque. She's almost floating, trance-like, a swarm of women behind her, and she calls out, "*Allah meri ammi ko jannat naseeb kare.*" God, grant my mother Heaven.

I have been trying to stay present. Centered. To not borrow worry while Mahmoud is in Gaza, but I allow my mind to wander into the unknown of the future. What if this will be me? What if Mahmoud dies there? I imagine he would be buried there in the Holy Land—perhaps in a mass grave, maybe in those blue body bags I've seen on Instagram with what look like zip ties on the ankles, his name in Arabic scrawled somewhere over it.

Will I find out from someone's post or someone's story, and will we have a *janaza* in absentia here, and will I have patience as the women buzz around me the way they are around my friend, consoling me, but in trying to do so, asking invasive questions about the manner of his death, perhaps blaming him? "Why did he go?" or blaming me, even to themselves: *Why didn't you stop him? What kind of wife are you?*

It's a tiresome day. My body is fatigued from the multiple trips up and down the stairs with Qasim, loading him and Maymuna in and out of car seats, bathing them. Qasim's last couple of naps have been mere minutes of shut-eye, and he and I are both spent. I rock him, holding him tight, trying to get him to stay on the pacifier that he constantly spits out and then wails for, wanting it back in. "You and I have both had a very hard day," I murmur in his ear before kissing his head.

I think back to a comment my mother made earlier in the day, after I had returned from the funeral. I had walked out of Qasim's room totally withered, in my third failed attempt to get him down.

"*Aaj bohot tang kar raha hai,*" she had called to me from the downstairs living room. He's being very bothersome today.

It's benign to her; I know it is. But to me, it feels like an indictment of my child's cries—decentering what he's saying and centering what she's feeling. Despite my own frustrations and fatigue, I know that Qasim crying is just him expressing his needs, and that Maymuna throwing a Cabbage Patch doll at Qasim isn't her being *taiz*—sly. It's her being two.

"This is what babies do," I say, in a feeble attempt to normalize my son's crankiness.

I sense in my mother an impatience that has encumbered her for as long as I can remember, but one I can also identify within me, and perhaps one that every mother struggles with at one point or another. Yet I also know that one poor choice does not become the entirety of a person's being, so I try to extend grace—to my kids, to my mother, and to myself.

I'm not limitless. I told Maymuna just minutes ago that my patience was wearing thin, and she had to get into her Pull-Up *now*. I acknowledge my limits with myself and with my children, and by doing so, I can reach into myself in time to say, *Take a break. Take a minute. Show up better.*

My children are not shrewd, bothersome, or inconvenient. They are children being children, entrusted to me as an *amana*. And all the things we ask of Allah are the things we have the opportunity to exercise most intimately as parents: compassion, forgiveness, mercy.

My children have needs, and I am tasked with practicing compassion.

My children push me to my limits, and that increases me in patience.

My children have cultivated my endurance. Carrying them in pregnancy—the relentless nausea, whole months when taking a step was painful, so much swelling that even my fingertips hurt, the total submission of my body, the helplessness and dependency I felt—and bringing them into the world was brutal, and at the same time, it strengthened me.

It strikes me sometimes while looking at my children after they've gone to sleep, or when we are all driving somewhere together, how blessed we are. I tell Mahmoud: "I think we are living that *dua* where everyone says, 'May Allah make your children the coolness of your eyes.'" Their health, their innocence, their very existence increases me in gratitude.

Mahmoud's call was to go, and mine was to stay. My acceptance of motherhood has indeed taken priority. And perhaps it is in the time I am alone with them, for however long it is, that my limits are extended, that I am made better.

Mahmoud does sleep for most of the flight to Cairo. But for a few minutes, he also does some thinking about how he got here. Since the genocide began, some days he has found it difficult to care for patients at work. All he can think about are the sick and the dying in Gaza. All he has been able to do is pray for their oppression to end.

Until he learns that that's not all he's able to do.

A few days before Ramadan starts, he wakes up too late to make it to Fajr at the mosque four minutes from our house. He goes anyway, and he runs into Abdullah Fateh, his old Hajj buddy. Abdullah is an emergency room (ER) doctor now, and Mahmoud is a hospitalist with fellowship training in wound care.

Abdullah tells Mahmoud he is leaving for Gaza, and that he will reach out if he has any wound care questions while he is there. Mahmoud is overwhelmed with respect for him and is honored at even the prospect of being able to help indirectly. He asks Abdullah to put him in touch with the nonprofit that is arranging the mission.

Two nights before Mahmoud is set to leave, Maymuna vomits in her crib. He gets Maymuna cleaned up while I work on cleaning everything else—her crib sheet, her stuffed flamingo, her pajamas. I lay out a plastic tablecloth around her crib to catch anything if it happens again. We work in a silent rhythm, each knowing our roles without having to speak at all. It took two last time Maymuna had a GI bug, and it takes two again. He wonders what it would be like if this happened two days after he left, instead of two days before, and he thanks God he could help care for his sick child here before leaving to care for sick children in Gaza.

Mahmoud loves being a father more than anything in the world—there is just no better feeling. To face the possibility of sacrificing that is painful, and Mahmoud realizes, in a new way, that was what Prophet Ibrahim (*alayhi al-salam*) was asked to do.

"I don't fear death per se," Mahmoud says to me the following day while stroking a febrile Maymuna's sweaty hair. "What I fear is not seeing the kids ever again, if the difference makes sense." It does. It's his experience of fatherhood that Mahmoud has placed at the altar of sacrifice.

Maymuna is so tired that she takes her afternoon nap on Mahmoud. He cherishes her resting on him; he knows it is helping her heal. He feels honored to be a source of comfort for another person. That is why he chose to follow in Abdullah's footsteps. So many things have lined up to enable to him to go to Gaza—the trip he took in 2009, getting into medical school, his fellowship in wound care. Now, Maymuna and Qasim are both a part of his motivation and also the pieces of himself he leaves behind.

Day 3: Monday, March 25

In Cairo, after *tarawih*, Mahmoud meets one of the former directors of European Hospital. He's one of many who have fled Gaza and are now living in Egypt, doing what they can from afar to send in medical supplies and help sustain the hospital they once headed.

Mahmoud is about to start the journey from Cairo to Rafah. The actual time shown on Google Maps is five and a half hours, but it will take somewhere between twelve and sixteen with the checkpoints.

He takes the last warm shower he expects to have for some time, then opens a pack of the cozy wool socks I bought for him before he left. Fresh socks—the gift his mother always gave him at the start of Ramadan. She didn't wait for Eid; they got them at the start of the month so that they wouldn't showcase thread-bare socks with holes in them to the entire congregation while in *sujud*. Brilliant.

The drive passes uneventfully, other than the desert flies that land on his legs every now and then. They take him back to his first trip to Gaza fifteen years ago. Their convoy drives down the middle lane, flanked by hundreds of aid trucks parked on either side of the road—miles and miles of stopped trucks carrying aid whose entry into Gaza has been blocked by Israel. Every so often they pass through a military checkpoint guarded by men with machine guns standing in booths, but none step onto the bus.

Everyone around Mahmoud is calm, so he tries to stay calm too. But he's not. He's just accepted being scared.

When they arrive at the Egyptian side of the Rafah border crossing and are awaiting further instructions, Mahmoud sends me some pictures of all the bags and boxes the convoy has assembled. Among the clearly marked boxes of medical supplies and a few boxes that say "Coffee for Gaza," I spot a couple of bright-pink cheetah-print suitcases, and I chuckle slightly to myself at the levity that can be found even in moments like these. I imagine perhaps they were from one of the children of another physician who is volunteering with Mahmoud, maybe stuffed with clothes that the kids themselves had selected to donate; or perhaps they were among some spare suitcases collecting dust in one of the doctors' attics. The plan is, after all, to leave the suitcases behind for the locals to use when they are inevitably displaced again.

"Lol at the pink cheetahs. What's their story?" I text Mahmoud.

My smile quickly fades at his reply, and I feel ill. "Someone in Egypt donated children's burial shrouds. Like five hundred of them. They're in those bags."

Mahmoud tells me Abdullah and a few others are going to the north by armored UN vehicle. The knots in my stomach tighten further. I am so worried about them. The raid on al-Shifa Hospital in the north is ongoing. Patients are being shot in their hospital beds. Physicians are being handcuffed and summarily executed.

Just a few months ago, Israel was trying to blame Hamas for their attacks on hospitals; their new script is that Hamas is using hospitals as a base. But their "terrorist tunnels" propaganda has been so successful that they don't even bother anymore. It is commonplace now for Israel to besiege and bombard hospitals all over Gaza, and not even my physician colleagues seem to be batting an eye.

When the raid on al-Shifa first started the week before Mahmoud left, he asked me, "What should I do if they raid the hospital I am in?"

"Do what everyone else is doing," I said. I remembered those fabric scissors by my senior overalls, the ones I had been using to cut the letters out to stitch onto the pants. I had caught sight of them as one of the men who robbed us pushed me along into my closet with my arm around my back, and I imagined fighting him off, breaking free, and defending myself with those scissors. I look at Mahmoud pointedly. "Definitely don't do something dumb like reach for one of the soldiers' guns."

As soon as he's on the Palestinian side of the border, Mahmoud tells me that the team lead was not allowed to cross. He doesn't know why. The Israelis won't let him in, and he'll try again tomorrow, and that's just how these things work.

Oh, and by the way, European Hospital is full now, so Mahmoud and the others may go to another hospital farther north, but not *the* north, just closer to the center of the strip in Deir al-Balah.

I feel whiplash. I don't understand. The plan was European Hospital, and only European Hospital, and that plan seems to be falling apart already. A few more of the volunteers are facing further danger going north, the lead isn't allowed in, the rest are being rerouted to another hospital. Is this a trap?

And I know the hospital Mahmoud is talking about.

"It's Shuhada al-Aqsa, isn't it?" I message him. I'd heard about that hospital in one of Mahmoud's initial phone calls, back when he was gathering information about joining a medical mission, and I remember finding it an interesting choice of name for a hospital. The Martyrs of al-Aqsa. Not the name you'd expect for a hospital from which you hope to leave alive.

"Let's just stick to calling it al-Aqsa," he says.

Yet there is also something deeply metaphorical about the name. It lies in such stark contrast to the Western matrix that Mahmoud and I trained in as young doctors, full of waste, over-consumption, and *israf*—excess. All of life is tracking toward death, and yet American society prefers not to live with this certainty, characterizing reminders of death as morbidly shocking, while the health-care system here has everyone clamoring until the very end to avoid it.

Elsewhere, circumstances are different; the reality and nearness of death are not only unavoidable, but not even considered something to *be* avoided. Every soul must taste death, and to die as a *shahid* is an honor, not a waste, not a life cut short or a fate that could have been circumvented. Of course the hospital honors those about whom the Quran says, "Think not of those who are slain in the way of Allah as dead. Nay, they are living, and with their Lord they have provision" (Quran 3:169).

So perhaps it would be an honor for Mahmoud to serve there instead.

At the border crossing, Mahmoud catches word of a possible ceasefire. His initial plan was to wait for a ceasefire to go to Gaza, and it feels like a *dua* answered that he made the intention to go regardless, and that he is now greeted with one. It is a short-lived hope though, as he learns that it was only a UN resolution. Everyone in Palestine knows that these resolutions, and really all of international law, are essentially meaningless to Israel and its offensive.

The journey to the hospital is silent and eerie. Outside there is utter darkness, with fires alongside the empty road every few meters and people huddled around them for warmth. Rafah is all tents and no space, and Mahmoud is brokenhearted at the sight. He wants to record it, to document it, but he doesn't want the Gazans to feel like he's treating it as if it were a zoo.

They don't mind ogling him though. They can tell he is not local, but when they ask, "*Kaifek*?"—How are you? and he replies, "Alhamdulillah," they are prompted to ask if he is Palestinian—just from the pronunciation of that one phrase.

Mahmoud isn't. He is Jordanian by way of Syria. But he does have one tie to Palestine: his grandmother on his mother's side was born in Haifa. His great-grandfather had moved there and started a business, which was burned to the ground during the Nakba, and his fourteen-year-old grandmother fled to Damascus hidden on a truck of watermelons. She died without ever returning to her childhood home, which remains occupied by Israeli settlers to this day.

Mahmoud and the others make their way through what he describes as an apocalyptic scene: barefoot children, starving animals, makeshift tents assembled from torn, stained sheets, people everywhere, trash everywhere. He sends me a picture of their *suhur*–several of them are sitting on the ground, and placed in the center is a communal plate of dates, some hummus, and a stack of pita bread. They will not eat or drink for the next fourteen hours. Not even genocide has interrupted the Palestinians observing the Ramadan fast, and the volunteers follow their lead.

When he gets to European Hospital, where he will be until it's time to leave for al-Aqsa Hospital in the morning, Mahmoud shares with me in a voice note small but vivid details of what he is seeing around him: every single one of the papers in the charts by the patients' beds has a bloodstain, there aren't enough supplies to fully sedate all the intubated ICU patients, so many are moaning and in restraints. In the background of his voice note I can hear the drones buzzing, and in the next note, the bombs start. I hear some concerned whispering among the men, but all the while, despite the drones and the bombs, the birds never stop chirping.

Day 4: Tuesday, March 26

Mahmoud is starting to feel a little useless, and therefore restless. He left home Saturday afternoon; it's now Tuesday morning, and he has little to show for his efforts thus far. The only meaningful thing he feels he's done has been giving some oranges he grabbed from the airport lounge to a local child and seeing his face break into a smile; the boy had not had fresh fruit in nearly six months.

One of the American orthopedic surgeons on the mission takes Mahmoud to the operating room at European Hospital; Mahmoud has volunteered to be his OR nurse until they have to leave for Deir al-Balah. On the way there, they are stopped by two physicians who ask them if they have a neurosurgeon on their team—they are in need of one urgently. Mahmoud and his companion apologize, telling them that the team is about to leave for al-Aqsa Hospital, but there is a local neurosurgeon who is just about to finish a case and should be available to them soon. Then Mahmoud has an idea. He walks the two physicians back to Dr. Shamisa, a neurosurgeon from Canada who had been a part of a medical mission in Benghazi during the war in Libya, where he operated on young men who'd been methodically shot in such a way as to be left alive, but quadriplegic. He is sleeping on a blanket on the floor of the cramped dormitory. Mahmoud nudges him awake.

Dr. Shamisa jumps up, happy to be of service. The other doctors tell him about the patient: a seven-year-old boy who has arrived from a field hospital intubated, whose brain matter is currently exposed. One pupil is reactive, the other isn't.

Dr. Shamisa rushes out of the dormitory with them and says he needs to see the CT scan. Mahmoud accompanies him to the radiology room, and as the child's scan is loading, Dr. Shamisa is approached by someone seeking his opinion on another patient's scan. He concludes both need surgery urgently if they are to have a chance of survival. The local neurosurgeon is not yet done with his case, but Dr. Hasan, the Jordanian neurosurgeon on this mission, *is* available.

"But if both of you are operating . . . We can't go to al-Aqsa without a neurosurgeon," Mahmoud says. These are the decisions made in settings such as this, and Dr. Shamisa reassures him that he'll find a way to al-Aqsa eventually.

My sister Sarah has arranged for drop-in iftars of one or two friends at a time over the next few evenings while Mahmoud is away. She knows me well; I'm an introvert and could probably go the whole time without having anyone over. I also resist asking for help, so I probably wouldn't plan a meal caravan myself.

The first of them is tonight, and one of my friends who comes is an anthropologist. We get to talking about her experience growing up as a Pakistani woman in the United Arab Emirates before moving to the States. She was an English teacher for adults there one summer, but as far as they knew she was from America, as that was where she was now residing.

One day she wore a Pakistani top, and one of her Arab pupils asked her where the top was from. When she said it was from

Pakistan, the woman asked if that was where she was from too. She said she was Pakistani, yes, and the woman refused to continue in her class after that—she was not going to be learning English from some Pakistani.

The racism that South Asians, especially expatriate workers, experience in the UAE has long been an open secret. I think of the racism inherent in the Palestinian story too. I learned more from Mahmoud about the different cultures among Arabs: the North Africans compared to the *Khalijis* (Gulf Arabs) compared to the *Shamis* (Levantine Arabs). To the West, though, they are all the same, and so why on earth can't those pesky native Palestinians simply comply and go to some other Arab country and give the Israelis a little more room? It is an outrageous and racist concept to its core, conceived and perpetuated by the British and the Americans, one that has spread into a toxic cancer of dehumanization. It permeates the architecture of language too. Arabs are never killed by Israelis; they die passively in an air strike, as if it fell spontaneously from the skies. The order of verbiage must follow an unspoken rule—it only makes sense to the West for the subject before the verb "kill" to be "Arabs."

Mahmoud's notes arrive late at night, just as I am getting ready to sleep, or at least lying in bed pretending I'll be able to. The fifteen-minute journey to al-Aqsa Hospital takes an hour and a half, and they're packed like sardines in a car that, "no, Samaiya, it's not armored. It has two shot-out windows." They zigzag through barefoot children in tattered clothing to arrive at al-Aqsa Hospital and meet with the director, Dr. Hasan. While many other hospital directors have evacuated, he has stayed, despite an air strike in which he was flung across a room, landing on—and breaking—his back. Dr. Hasan's wife and kids were killed in that air strike, and he can no longer bend in *ruku* or *sujud* while in prayer. This man, who has lost so much and remains in chronic physical and emotional pain, welcomes Mahmoud and the other volunteers and serves them coffee.

They have wrapped up the Fajr prayer, and Mahmoud is about to take a nap before getting back to his work at al-Aqsa later in the morning. I inquire more about his first day there. He tells me the hospital is filled from top to bottom with displaced families. They, along with the local physicians and staff and their own families, are all living within the hospital walls. The wards are filled with four times the usual number of patients—far beyond capacity. There is absolutely no space to even spread one's elbows. There is nothing but refugees, emaciated donkeys, dirt- and dust-covered children, and patients with external fixators—devices made of pins and rods, used in cautious optimism that complex leg fractures from being crushed by rubble may have a chance of mending rather than requiring amputation. He's never seen so many of them in his life.

I ask him what medical care he'll be providing there, and he tells me 90% of the injuries are blast injuries. These are not the wounds he treats in the US, which are mostly chronic wounds like diabetic foot ulcers. In Gaza, limbs are shredded. Sometimes he can see the ground through a hole in a patient's arm or leg. Mahmoud will mainly be taking care of shrapnel wounds so extensive that dressing changes have to be done under conscious sedation because of the pain, and stump wounds from amputation sites that aren't healing due to poor nutrition and unsanitary conditions—dirty floors, open sewage, flies and mosquitoes everywhere.

Despite all this, Mahmoud says he's in a good headspace. I ask him what it is that's helping, and he tells me that the patients amaze him with their steadfastness and their strength.

Before he left, he told me, "I think they will give me more than I give them."

I understand now.

His observations are about the recitation of the Quran, the verses they choose and the way they recite. He sees that the food scarcity has not impacted their fasting whatsoever, and prayers continue, only shortened so that the staff may be ready for the next emergency. He talks of Bachar, one of the locals he is paired with. Israel has killed thirty of his family members, yet he continues his work, unpaid, as he has for the last six months. Just like dozens of other Bachars who are doing the same.

They are people who persist. People who have a beautiful patience.

Day 5: Wednesday, March 27

It becomes a sort of split existence for me; I feel like I'm living in two dimensions. In the first, I continue my own job in clinical operations while trying to ignore how insignificant my work feels compared to Mahmoud's. I haven't told any of my coworkers what Mahmoud is doing; my boss knows only that he is on a "work trip." I don't want polite sympathies or political judgments, and I'm fairly new in my role, so I don't want any biases about the quality of my work either.

After the nanny leaves for the day, I spend the afternoons with Maymuna and Qasim at the park, at the mosque, anywhere out of the house and away from its reminders of Mahmoud's absence. Dinner, bath, bedtime. The kids are doing much better than I expected, and I am too. I keep my patience with them. I tap into a physical strength I didn't know I had.

I start to rationalize my anxiety about Mahmoud's safety. Practically speaking, this trip is coordinated by the WHO with the IDF; they have his and all the foreign medical staff's location, which is meant to reassure me that they won't kill him. I imagine having an American passport helps some. And Abdullah went, came back, and has gone again.

But those logistical facts don't put me more at ease. I am relying on Allah alone. I feel in my bones that Mahmoud will be OK, whether or not he survives.

I don't fear his death. Not because it is not a possibility, but because in some time, in some place, it is an inevitability. One of the verses Mahmoud told me the Palestinians recite often now is: "Death will overtake you no matter where you may be, even inside lofty towers" (Quran 4:78).

I cling to this in the hours between putting the kids down for bed and waiting to receive a note from him that tells me he's lived another day. Sometimes his messages don't come until the middle of the night; I keep my phone nearby and sleep with one eye open—as I did in the days Qasim was a tiny newborn—making sure that I don't miss the faintest proof of life.

In the second dimension, I am in Gaza with Mahmoud. Hearing the drones in the background of his videos feels different from hearing them in the Instagram profiles of Motaz and Plestia and Bisan.

Mahmoud tells me another night has passed, and he has seen patients who came in because a talking drone entered their house and started spraying tiny bullets everywhere, like something out of *The Terminator*, and that the wounds he is seeing are horrific and extensive. Today there was a double amputation, and when he went to clean someone's wound, he was greeted by a colony of maggots. And despite the UN ceasefire resolution, each night the bombings have become more frequent. And tonight is the loudest one yet.

And so when I am pulled back into the first dimension the next day by my neighbor at the park asking me about my weekend plans and telling me about her upcoming move, I want to scream at the top of my lungs, *Why are we talking about anything other than Palestine?*

I tell Mahmoud my back hurts from bending over the bathtub to bathe the kids, a task he usually does. Mahmoud tells me his back hurts from bending over the patients, as their beds don't rise. We have a laugh about our sameness, though I feel pain for the ones on the beds. They are the most tested.

Mahmoud took part in a disarticulation procedure today on Raed, a patient whose wound had become too infected to spare any of the limb. It was an unfortunate procedure where the entire femur had to be removed from the pelvis, rendering the chance of a prosthesis nearly impossible, leaving him to use crutches for life. Without the surgery, Raed would have become septic and likely died. There was no alternative. When Mahmoud asked for his consent for the amputation, Raed agreed to the surgery and said, "I have given this leg *fi sabilillah*, and will be reunited with it in Jannah." He was tearful, but he submitted to Allah's will, and this is the theme Mahmoud sees time and time again. The people are heartbroken at the loss of limbs and loved ones, but they accept Allah's will with an unshakeable conviction, saying *hasbun Allahu wa ni'mal wakil*—Sufficient for us is Allah and He is the best Disposer of Affairs.

The time for iftar comes while in the surgery to remove Raed's femur, and someone slips a date into Mahmoud's mouth under his mask.

At home and in Gaza, there are bright spots. I catch from the corner of my eye Qasim on his play mat, flat on his belly. "You rolled over! You rolled over, Qasim!" I squeal. I turn him on his back. "Do it again, bubs," I say, hoping to record a video for Mahmoud. He doesn't, of course. I should have learned by now that my kids never do it for the camera.

Meanwhile, Mahmoud tells me he's met so many Mahmouds, more than he's ever met in his life. He tells me about Khidr, who graduated from medical school in Cairo and is working, essentially, as a volunteer now. Khidr was just about to call it quits before Mahmoud arrived, but now he is eagerly learning about wound care, wanting to absorb every last shred of knowledge Mahmoud has to impart. He tells me about Abdelkarim, a second-year orthopedic resident whom he first thought was on something because he talked so fast, and how his debridements have gotten gentler, and how he looks forward to working with him because he's so funny.

In the evening, after the doctors break their fast, they sit together over Arabic coffee, sharing stories, and Mahmoud breaks out the bag of dark chocolate covered espresso beans he bought from Sprouts the morning before he left. Their smiles widen at the treat (chocolate has been banned from Gaza by Israel for years). He feels a sense of belonging there, not just in these moments with the staff, but when he is caring for the patients too.

"You know what they tell me, Samaiya?" he sends in a message at night. He writes it in Arabic, the language of Amman, his birthplace. "*Nahnu wa iyyakum wahid.*"

"What's it mean?" I ask, and the two gray check marks appear right away and turn blue. I see that he is typing in real time.

"We and you are one."

Day 6: Thursday, March 28

Mahmoud continues to work with his protégés today. Abdelkarim, bless his heart, can be so aggressive with the pus pockets; he pushes at one abscess too hard and it bursts open, exploding pus all over Mahmoud's arms and onto his scrubs. Abdelkarim can't help but laugh, and Mahmoud, disgruntled as he is, joins in too. He bonds with Khidr too; Khidr has been diligent in learning which wound care supplies are best used for different types of wounds, and Mahmoud is letting him do more of the debridements to apply his newfound knowledge.

Homesickness starts to tug at him, though it's a peculiar kind. Mahmoud doesn't miss the creature comforts of our house—his bed, his shower, air conditioning. He is homesick only for us. And he is worried I'm not being more forthcoming with him about how hard solo parenting is, worried that the kids miss him too much, but also worried that they don't notice his absence at all.

He sees Maymuna and Qasim everywhere, in all the little babies and toddlers in Gaza. He wishes he could see the patients during the day, and then come home to me and the kids in the evening to do bedtime, to help put them to sleep. Or rather, that we were there with him, all together in a safer, happier Gaza.

A young girl is being wheeled into the MSF (Doctors Without Borders) clinic, and Mahmoud doesn't want to look when he sees that she's close to Maymuna's age. She looks so worn. He doesn't want to see which of her limbs is missing. He brings himself to evaluate her, and she has both legs, alhamdulillah, but one is in an external fixator. These have so often failed and resulted in an amputation. He makes *dua* for her: "Ya Allah, please spare her leg."

Where there's a Maymuna, there's also a Qasim—a baby Yaman, whom the other doctors were going to turn away because they haven't been seeing pediatric patients, only adults. It turns out Yaman's ailment is a straightforward one. He has a bad diaper rash, with satellite lesions everywhere. Diapers are two dollars apiece, and his mother had been forced to use one diaper a day. When the rash started, some refugees in the next tent over recommended steroid cream, which only made the rash worse. Mahmoud hands Yaman's mother a tub of Desitin and some nystatin powder. She receives it happily and mentions someone she wants to share it with in her camp.

Insomnia, a phenomenon I don't routinely experience, begins to rear its head. Even though I lived alone for two years, I lost the ability to sleep deeply by myself after I married Mahmoud. When he has been away—for night shifts, for guys' trips—the struggle to sleep has plagued me. Much of it is remnants from the home invasion. I can't confine myself to the corner of the house where our bedroom is located; I need to be in the middle, in the open, able to hear every tap on the door. Since having kids, I have become even more vigilant; there comes a subconscious need to stand watch at night, to be close to their rooms so as not to miss a nighttime wake-up—or worse. I settle for the couch in our upstairs loft.

But this is the longest Mahmoud has been away, and it's catching up to me, this disjointed sleep. By 5:00 p.m., I can hardly stand. I want nothing more than to lie down on Maymuna's play couch, but she wants to jump, or play dinosaurs, or sweep her mini mop over my feet, and Qasim always wants to cuddle.

I walk my kids over to my dear friend who lives across the street from me and ring her bell. She opens the door. "I need a nap," I say. She pulls Maymuna into her entryway, then takes Qasim from my arms.

"Say no more," she says, nonplussed. I trudge back inside my own house and fall asleep on our bed for the first time since Mahmoud left, the late afternoon sun warming my back. Only guilt wakes me after forty-five minutes. I can't leave my kids longer than that. I can't accept too much help.

It's my sister Sarah's turn to bring a friend to break their fast with me tonight, and they're coming with their families so that Maymuna can spend some time with her cousins and friends. Over dinner, one of the husband's best friends comes up; I remember him from their wedding years ago and have seen him at birthday parties and such since. He is Jewish, and I ask if the two of them can talk about Palestine, or if it's easier to avoid the topic altogether.

"His wife did reach out when all this started," our friend says.

"All this." It's the polite phrasing we use to refer to what's happening in Palestine: a seventy-five-year battle over indigenous land, the start of a new colony by white men who hold the power to redraw borders and rename countries, and the violent expansionism and unfettered imperialism that continues to this day.

They ask me how Mahmoud is doing and gush about how inspiring it is that while most people evacuate from a combat zone, Mahmoud ran right in, fearless. I want to tell them that he isn't fearless at all, and that, as Nelson Mandela—who was himself considered a terrorist by the US until only fifteen years ago—said: "Courage isn't the absence of fear, but rather the triumph over it."

I instead repeat to them all the things I've told myself: The IDF has his coordinates, their trip is under the coordination of the WHO, yada, yada. I also want to tell them that when I had recited this same litany of reassurances to Sakeena, Abdullah's wife, she reminded me that the IDF has shot babies in the head, and that there is a roster of a thousand or more children who have a "0" as their age in the death registry, infants who never even reached toddlerhood, infants born and killed during the siege. My brother-in-law says that having a US passport should help; it has to help. I've let myself think that before too, only to remember Rachel Corrie, who also had a US passport and was bulldozed by the IDF in 2003 while protesting the expanding settlements, a death that was simply written off as an "accident" by the Israeli army and that the US never even bothered to investigate.

At 8:30 p.m., Maymuna, an introvert like me, announces that she is tired and wants to lie down. I put her to bed and linger a little in the quiet of her room. These bedtimes now anchor me; instead of feeling burdensome or monotonous as they previously have at times, they let me breathe in the present moment, where things can still follow a predictable routine.

Sarah and our friend, along with their husbands, generously offer to stay back so that I can go to the mosque for *tarawih*. With no one else at the house at night while my kids are asleep, I haven't been able to go at all this Ramadan. What a blessing it is to spend some part of the night listening to the young *qari*'s recitation, to move alongside my fellow Muslims in *ruku,* to press my head against the soft turquoise carpet in *sujud,* and to be in Allah's home rather than my own. I whisper my *dua* into my cupped hands, "Please, Allah, end the suffering of the people in Gaza, and please give me the patience You've given them."

Day 7: Friday, March 29

Mahmoud and I carry on along parallel tracks, several hours apart.

My Day	Mahmoud's Day
4:30 a.m. – Qasim wakes up to feed, and I catch up on any of Mahmoud's overnight texts I may have missed. Qasim goes back to sleep, I pray Fajr, and, if I am lucky, I go back to sleep too	3:30 a.m. – Mahmoud has *suhur*, which usually consists of canned tuna, dates, and pita bread, then he prays Fajr and rests before his morning rush starts
7:30 a.m. – Maymuna and Qasim wake up and the morning rush starts	9:00 a.m. – The workday starts with *janaza* funeral prayers for all the patients who have died overnight
8:30 a.m. – The nanny arrives and takes Maymuna to Montessori while I start my workday	10:00 a.m. – Mahmoud begins work, which usually consists of debridements, pain control, burn care, and amputations

My Day	Mahmoud's Day
5:00 p.m. – I finish up work, the nanny leaves, and I take the kids out somewhere	6:00 p.m. – Mahmoud ends his workday with Asr, then rests until iftar
6:30 p.m. – Dinner, bath, and bedtime routine, sometimes with the help of "the virtual babysitter" (screen time) for Maymuna while I get Qasim down, or inadvertent sleep training for Qasim while I get Maymuna down	8:00 p.m. – The staff break their fast together, and then the drones start, followed by the F-16s, and then the bombs
8:00 p.m. – My own dinner after the kids are down, followed by what I affectionately call nighttime rounds, where I check on the kids as they sleep peacefully and I count my million blessings that they do so under a sky of stars and not bombs	10:00 p.m. – Mahmoud does his nighttime rounds with the patients, where he checks on how they've been doing since he saw them in the morning
9:00 p.m. – I catch up with Mahmoud after he's had *suhur* and prayed Fajr	11:00 p.m. – Mahmoud catches up with the staff over espresso beans and sends me a daily update of his thoughts and observations

People on my social media keep referring to a ceasefire, but Mahmoud tells me the bombs fall all night. Each day I receive a message saying that today's bombs were the loudest ones yet.

Today Mahmoud tells me he gave away Maymuna's outgrown shoes, the little Vans with sequined rainbows, and the gray sweater with the orange vinyl flower and a corona of pink glitter. It hurts to give it away, he says; he remembers seeing Maymuna in it. I tell him, "*Ya Abu Maymuna*, it hurts you to part with Maymuna's clothes and shoes. I cannot imagine the grief of the parents who have to part with their actual child."

He also says Raed, the man who had the disarticulation procedure two days ago, is not doing too well. He survived the surgery, but Mahmoud worries that they've taken out all the tissue they could. There's nothing left to remove, so sepsis would be a death sentence. He is worried Raed won't survive, not from a lack of trying, but from the horrendous lack of resources.

I think about the people of Palestine as victims of a systematic, sustained home invasion. Much of the world has suddenly noticed their plight, but this genocide is only the latest phase of that invasion. It has been ongoing for decades. The trauma is generational. And Israel's is not the kind of home invasion where they invade, pillage, and leave. These people have settlers who invade the home and stay in it, or worse, who bomb the home, killing mother, father, sister, and leaving behind only baby brother, or, worse still, kill everyone and destroy everything in a one-mile radius, leaving behind only a crater.

Those who escape death or grievous bodily harm remain emotionally injured. The children pulled out of the crumbled buildings alive, or the ones whose families have not yet been bombed at all—they, too, are injured. Mahmoud has another patient who hasn't required much wound care, but whose eyes are empty. He is a child who has seen too much. Sometimes he looks at his family and doesn't even recognize them.

I wonder if all the calls for a ceasefire are successful, and if the siege finally ends, what will happen afterward? How do a people recover from this kind of decimation? How do a child's eyes that have beheld the sight of shredded parents and a destroyed home ever look bright again?

Day 8: Saturday, March 30

While I no longer practice clinically, I have a continuing medical education course at the hospital on the weekend, one that I signed up for anticipating Mahmoud to be off and with the kids, but now falls while he is away. I don't have childcare on the weekends. If it were one child, maybe I could ask one of my neighbors, but I have a toddler and an infant. It's too big a favor.

The anxiety in my stomach bubbles up as I call my mother. I know she will help me, but somewhere within me I wonder if I am the bothersome child, the one crying for "mama" when I should be able to figure it out on my own. I try to have everything situated as best I can before going to the hospital. Are diapers changed? Is everyone fed and rested? I put Maymuna in her crib and rush out before she is even asleep. I have to time it so I can be back before she wakes up.

A month ago was the worst of the fighting, Khidr and Bachar tell Mahmoud. Khidr remembers the disorientation—thinking it was time for Maghrib and then checking his watch only to see that it was the middle of the night. Two out of every three patients were dying at that time; that was when Bachar lost his mother, father, and siblings. Mahmoud is surprised and somewhat ashamed not to have known while here in the US how much things had escalated, but it is partly a function of how many journalists have been killed. There are few left to report from the ground, and what they do transmit certainly isn't making headline news on CNN or Fox News. It is buried halfway through the paper in small print and reported daily as isolated incidents: a hospital here, a school there, a couple dozen people killed. There is no cohesive narrative that asks, isn't this an awful lot of days? Isn't this the tenth time a hospital has been struck?

Mahmoud notices that the way doctors obtain a medical history is different than here. There isn't the guessing game of "What happened to you?" There is only "How long ago did they bomb you?"—and when the patient answers, they relay both when they were injured and how many died alongside them.

I come home from the hospital to a completely dysregulated Maymuna. She convinced my mother she didn't need a nap. She demanded more Medjool dates—the fat, sweet kind—and she had six of them. She's pumped full of sugar, and tired, and missing her father, and she is a mess.

I sigh, close my eyes, and stroke my thumb and forefinger over my eyebrows and around my temples. "Thanks, Mom," I say.

"You sure you'll be OK?" she asks on her way out the door.

Qasim is clinging to me, and I hear Maymuna wailing "Baba!" while sprawled out on the kitchen floor. "Yeah, yeah, I'll be OK. Thank you so much."

It is the first of the odd nights at the end of Ramadan, and the search for Laylat al-Qadr has begun. I try to look on the bright side; getting the kids down early tonight means I can settle onto my prayer mat and talk to Allah of my struggle.

There is a night that is better than Laylat al-Qadr tucked away like a secret within a lesser-known hadith: "Ibn Umar related that the Prophet ﷺ said, 'Shall I tell you about a night that is even better than Laylat al-Qadr? It is a night in which a guard keeps watch [*ribat*] in a dangerous place, knowing not whether he will return to his family'" (*al-Bayhaqi, al-Hakim, al-Nasa'i*).

According to another hadith, "To stand watch [*ribat*] for one hour in the way of God is better than standing in prayer near the Black Stone on Laylat al-Qadr" (*Ibn Hibban, al-Bayhaqi*). It's a powerful statement that service to the community can reach the level of or even exceed the meritoriousness of private worship.

That night, Mahmoud and his friends—the staff are now all friends—gather for iftar: Khidr, Abdelkarim, and Dr. Nasir and Dr. Malek, two of the Gazan surgeons. Mahmoud has been told repeatedly by many, many of the Palestinians that they wish the situation were better so they could host the doctors properly as guests. Dr. Nasir serves coffee—the Al Ameed Arabic coffee Mahmoud brought from the US and had given him to drink with his own family. The conversation turns to the *murabitun*—the ones in *ribat* standing guard like those in the hadith.

They discuss that there are three categories of people in Gaza:

♦ People who want to leave Gaza and have the means, or plan to obtain the means

♦ People who do not want to leave Gaza despite having the means

+ The internally displaced, who do not have the means to
  leave, and are forced to move from place to place within
  Gaza (such as from the north to the south)

And then there is the reaction to those who leave. Some who
remain look down on them, but many don't blame them.

Dr. Nasir shares that his six-year-old daughter asked him
about the people who leave Gaza. "Are they the *murabitun?*" He
tells her no; this title is for those who stay. She proudly declares
to him, "Then I will not leave Gaza."

At this Khidr is near tears, in part because he is moved by the
boldness of Dr. Nasir's daughter, and in part because his mind
has gone to a friend of his who left Gaza for medical treatment.
He was in desperate need, and Khidr asks Dr. Nasir about him.
"He had to go."

Dr. Nasir placates Khidr, as if to advise him: Don't limit Allah's
mercy based on the concreteness of a child; He is al-Rahim (the
Merciful), and al-Basit (the Expander).

The night's bombings begin, and they are louder than usual.
Dr. Nasir can sense Mahmoud's unease. "These are a kilometer
away," Dr. Nasir reassures him. But they continue, and Mahmoud wonders if Dr. Nasir doesn't want him to know that they
are in fact closer.

Some thirty minutes later, a knock is heard on the door. Word
travels fast, and someone has come to let the doctors know that
a local shaykh has been identified as one of the martyrs.

"*La hawla wa la quwwata illa billah,*" Dr. Nasir says. There is
no might nor power except with Allah.

Before Mahmoud can ask more details about the shaykh—
how Dr. Nasir knows him, how old he is, does he have a family—the conversation continues as it was before they heard of

his passing. Death is so commonplace as to derail nothing. They are not desensitized; they are saddened, but resolute. There is no time anymore to be overcome with mourning before the martyrs arrive at the hospital's morgue.

Earlier in the night, Khidr and Mahmoud had inventoried what little remained of his supplies, which are still sitting out. Dr. Nasir's eyes land on the three-pack of cherry flavored Children's Motrin that we purchased from Costco before Mahmoud's trip; he picks it up and examines it, then sets it back down. "Good, this is good," he says. That's all he says, but Mahmoud knows what he means.

Palestinians have too much pride and too much reliance on Allah to beg, and neither Dr. Nasir nor Dr. Malek have ever asked for anything for themselves. A few days ago, a young girl came and tugged on Mahmoud's pants while he was in the courtyard of the hospital, begging for some money. Dr. Nasir was with Mahmoud, and he gently redirected her: "Ask from Allah, not from this man." But from his comment, Mahmoud surmises that one of Dr. Nasir's children is sick, and on his way out of the room, Mahmoud stacks one of the bottles of Children's Motrin on the box of coffee Dr. Nasir brought with him to serve.

Dr. Malek's ask is a similar non-ask: "Maybe my kids would enjoy this snack too." When I learn this, the guilt consumes me. He is referring to the trail mix I sent along for Mahmoud in small individual Ziplocs. I had packed only fifteen bags; I was tired on that last night before Mahmoud left, as I scooped peanuts, walnuts, chocolate chips, and raisins into bags in assembly-line fashion. Mahmoud has given some away at the iftars, and others, so as not to draw attention to this little indulgence, he has eaten stealthily in slivers of privacy that are near impossible to find in an overcrowded hospital that is housing doctors, patients, and everyone in between.

"I hope you gave him all the trail mix you had," I tell Mahmoud, when he shares this with me over text.

"I had only two bags left. I gave them both."

This is where I weep. I wish I could have sent a whole suitcase of trail mix, and then I wish that I had to send no trail mix at all, and that Dr. Malek and his family had their own homes and their own pantries and all the snacks their hearts and bellies desired.

Day 9: Sunday, March 31

Another Costco find, the black Hurley slip-on shoes Mahmoud had snapped up just as we were heading to the checkout line, to which I raised an eyebrow and told him the space was not worth it, turns out to be very much worth it; they end up being used by Khidr, whose shoe broke today. And to Abdelkarim goes Mahmoud's sleeping pad because he has had back pain for months from sleeping on a wooden frame. Unlike Dr. Nasir, who stays in the outpatient clinic building just across the courtyard, Abdelkarim lives farther out, about five hundred meters from the hospital, far enough to be vulnerable to an air strike during the simple act of walking home, so he chances a journey back and forth only once a week or so.

I know little about Abdelkarim, but I worry about him as he plans to go home for the day to spend time with his family. The IDF was just in his neighborhood looking for a man, and when he wasn't there, they took his wife. I don't know what will happen to Abdelkarim or whether Mahmoud will ever see him again.

I don't get any updates that night about how Mahmoud's final weekend at al-Aqsa Hospital is going. He typically messages me in the hour before I go to sleep, and we have a chance to text synchronously during that time. I stay awake waiting, but nothing comes, and then sleep overtakes me. When I wake up in the middle of the night to zero notifications, I ask him, "Are you sending me fewer updates because you're busier? More tired?" I don't hear anything back.

And then the next morning, while I am feeding Qasim, everything arrives at once:

"There are bombings close by so we just don't have service"

"The ER is already full"

"Very large bomb went off. It is the tent adjacent to the hospital"

"UK team came and said they have to evacuate the hospital"

"We got a shrapnel victim to the neck. Very close death"

"I don't know why my messages aren't getting through"

"General feeling around here is fear but we are still working"

"I'm sorry to put this on you"

"There was another air strike that was close"

"Now also MSF team evacuated"

"I hope my messages reach you at some point"

My stomach falls to my toes and I feel fear gripping me, tightening my chest, and coursing through my veins. I ask Mahmoud when he is being evacuated—he is being evacuated, right?

There's no response, only more messages about how Dr. Shamisa, the neurosurgeon, saw bombing victims close enough to identify the brain matter, the left lobe from the right lobe. I start searching on Instagram for news; it hasn't occurred to me the whole time Mahmoud has been away to check for updates about the area he is in on social media. Until now, my only news source has been him.

There it is—breaking news on Al Jazeera. An air strike on al-Aqsa in Deir al-Balah, on a tent in its compound; several people reported to be injured.

Seeing al-Aqsa Hospital's name in print on a news headline about an air strike feels unreal. It hits me like a bag of bricks that my husband is there, and my mind can't process the sequence of events. Which messages were written before the air strike, and which were sent after? Is Mahmoud still there at the hospital? That just had an air strike? Surely he is not still there. Of course he is there. Where else would he be? Are there more air strikes coming, or have they already come and are we simply awaiting news of the damage they've inflicted?

I am disoriented. A friend stayed the night at my house, and I suggest going to First Watch to eat. I look at their seasonal menu—that Hawaiian French toast sure sounds good—but then I realize how ridiculous it is to think that Mahmoud is safe enough that I could go out to a restaurant. How ashamed I feel that I could even think about treating myself amidst a genocide of my fellow humans, as if death weren't lurking so closely. As if the panic I feel for Mahmoud is not how everyone in Gaza has felt for months.

Everything remains confusing and silent this way for the next few hours. My friend is planning to go to a mothers' program at the mosque; maybe it will be good for me to go? I agree to join, thinking it might help distract me from sitting in my uncertainty. "Motherhood and Resilience" is the topic. I have little to say. What am I to say other than I am stretched like a rubber band to limits I didn't know were possible, and that I am trying to breathe resilience right now in this very moment.

I don't hear from Mahmoud again for another few hours. He's OK. The initial commotion has quelled. The drones are still present, but Mahmoud is told by staff who were at al-Shifa and have now come to al-Aqsa that this is significantly lighter than the raids that took place there.

Earlier that morning before the air strike, Mahmoud had seen some young men at the morgue crying over the body of their deceased mother, and he and the staff prayed her *janaza* in the very same courtyard where the air strike would occur. There was a child with a cleft palate prepped and ready for the plastic surgeon to start operating when the UK-Med team came in, helmets and vests on, to evacuate him. Khidr asked Mahmoud why they were not also evacuating him, and Mahmoud replied, "Because I am one of you."

Dr. Shamisa, Mahmoud tells me, wasn't relieved that the missile missed him. "It would have been an honor," he said. He has lived a full life, and he walks through the halls of the hospital as someone unafraid and ready, whenever the time comes, to meet his end. I also learn that when Mahmoud's messages weren't going through, Khidr took him up the stairwell close to the roof just so he could let me know he was OK, and once Mahmoud made it onto the roof, he realized how easy it would be to get sniped.

In the evening, after the kids are down, I reread Mahmoud's texts, listen again to his voice notes, pressing rewind on this day to live through it all over again. I can follow along now. There was an air strike this morning in Deir al-Balah, on a tent in the compound of al-Aqsa Hospital, in the courtyard where Mahmoud had just prayed *janaza* an hour before. He was one building behind the air strike. Dr. Shamisa was in the front of the building, closest to the courtyard, in the ICU. He was so close that the glass on the windows blew out. A patient in that same building who had been hospitalized from a previous air strike was struck in the neck by the shattered glass. He began bleeding profusely and was rushed immediately one building over to the OR, the OR that Mahmoud was next door to, completing a dressing change on Raed, who had the disarticulation a few days ago, who had given his leg for the sake of Allah, and who is now at risk of dying from sepsis. The staff pulled Mahmoud and Abdelkarim into the room with the patient whose neck was bleeding, to put pressure on it until the surgeon could come. But not the vascular surgeon, because there weren't any. It was a general surgeon who stitched him up, and the man survived. Four others were *shuhada.*

Day 10: Monday, April 1

The day after the air strike at al-Aqsa Hospital is Mahmoud's last day there. He starts to feel the heartache of parting ways; these people have grown from colleagues to friends and are family now. He worries about them, and he feels a sense of betrayal leaving them to return to his "real life."

My afternoon on that final day is spent at the park with Maymuna and Qasim, hoping that the next time we come here, it will be Mahmoud pushing Maymuna on the swing. I try to leave once the wind picks up and begins bothering Qasim, but Maymuna spots a yellow ball in someone's stroller and refuses to go. "It's hard to let go, mama," I tell her as she starts to get worked up. "Try it. Bye, ball!"

"Bye, ball!" she says, far more begrudgingly.

It is only after I manage to get them loaded into the back seat and am strapping myself in that I see Mahmoud's sister's texts:

"Have you heard from Mahmoud?"

"Another attack in Deir al-Balah. Foreign aid workers."

Mahmoud's older brother Omar had just graduated from nursing school a couple months before Mahmoud's mission to Gaza, and almost immediately after, he learned that his surgeon friend, Dr.

Jawad Khan, was planning to go too. Inspired by them both, he asks Dr. Jawad to take him along as his OR nurse.

Omar tells me before leaving that they will be at European Hospital, so I imagine that despite being a few miles apart—closer than they've been in six months—Mahmoud and Omar's paths may not cross at all. But he is convinced they will find a way.

At the Rafah border crossing, Omar sees a white man carrying some eggs. *That's interesting*, he thinks. He had imagined most of the volunteers to be Arab and carrying medical supplies, so the sight of a white person holding eggs sticks with him.

Omar, Jawad, and Athar, a neighbor who is one of Mahmoud's closest friends, are all on the same mission, and they manage to get to al-Aqsa Hospital as well. As soon as they do, they hear about the air strike in Deir al-Balah that was carried out just after they entered Gaza.

After loading the kids and reading the texts about the air strike on foreign aid workers in Deir al-Balah, I try to reach Mahmoud by WhatsApp call, but I can't. There's no connection. Or his phone is off. But this time, I don't break down as I did just yesterday with the al-Aqsa air strike. This time, I remain steadfast.

I have seen Palestinians lose their homes and their limbs. Dozens and dozens of loved ones have become thirty thousand lost, all with patient perseverance and reliance on God—and I have felt only the slightest possibility of losing one. Who am I to feel that my loss would be special? On the human scale of the universe, my Mahmoud is the same as their Mahmouds.

And so it is that even before I learn that it was a World Central Kitchen convoy the IDF targeted, that the aid workers' Australian, Polish, and British passports didn't spare them, that the man with the eggs whom Omar saw was one of the aid workers killed, that Mahmoud's convoy will leave just a few hours after that air strike, that he wound up crossing the Rafah border, then the Suez tunnel, and then departed from Cairo, and even before the plane lands and I pick him up from the airport and we embrace and I don't let him go—even before any of those things happen, I know with all the conviction I have that whether he survives his trip or not, Mahmoud is going to be OK. And I know that I will be too, because through this window opened into Gaza, the Palestinians have given me the gift of their own beautiful patience.

Day 11: Tuesday, April 2

After the bodies of the World Central Kitchen volunteers arrive to al-Aqsa Hospital, the news spreads quickly: foreign aid workers were killed. The Palestinians working in the hospital are deeply saddened by the fact that those who came to help them—those they honored as guests in their homeland—will not return to their own homes safely.

Mahmoud's last night in al-Aqsa overlaps with Omar, Jawad, and Athar's first. They pray *tarawih* together, and Mahmoud introduces his family and friends to everyone in the hospital so they can hit the ground running the next day. Jawad has Omar to translate for him, but Athar will need someone to help too. Mahmoud connects him with some medical students who speak both English and Arabic. I chuckle at this; once upon a time Athar was my attending when I was an intern fresh out of medical school on my internal medicine rotation, and I know he is a tough teacher. I wonder if Gaza will soften him, but I imagine it's more likely that he will demand the same of his students there, language barrier and combat zone notwithstanding.

The joy on Mahmoud's face at seeing his family and friends, for however little time, is visible in the photo I receive from his brother. It is the kind of smile I've seen when he is doing jiujitsu with his brothers, when he is in a place where he most belongs.

In the hospital that night they see a father walking alone, carrying his little child in a shroud. Following them is an intubated child on a stretcher with a missing left arm. This is the first sight the newcomers see, and it is the last image that stays with Mahmoud before he leaves for European Hospital.

Mahmoud has his final iftar with everyone over his favorite food—*fetteh jaaj*—at Dr. Nasir's home, and there he says goodbye to Dr. Malek and Khidr. He doesn't know the route the World Central Kitchen convoy took, nor whether their convoy will follow the same one. As he leaves early the next morning, he can see in the distance the dust hanging over the once-thriving neighborhood of Khan Younis. At a roundabout, a man asks to use their vehicle to help collect the bodies of his six brothers who have been killed—an impossible request that they must decline.

It's an immediate change of pace at European Hospital, which is a much bigger and more established hospital than al-Aqsa. There are more supplies and simply more hands to manage the workload there, though they, too, are bursting at the seams, absorbing the patient volume from all the smaller hospitals nearby that have been destroyed. Mahmoud's night there feels like lying in the lap of luxury—there is a fan, and no mosquitoes. He feels a little guilty at these accommodations, yet he would trade them in a heartbeat to go back and share in the struggle with his friends Dr. Nasir and Dr. Malek.

Mahmoud walks through the ICU to get the lay of the land for Mohamad Abdelfattah, his old friend from medical school and Team Intifada, who will arrive in three weeks from California. The very first patient he sees is the seven-year-old who Dr. Shamisa operated on the first day they were there, the one he stayed behind for. The young boy is still intubated, but his vitals are stable. He is alone. There is a bleak, newly created acronym for these children: WCNSF—wounded child, no surviving family.

Mahmoud has shed almost everything he brought with him. All the medical supplies, snacks, extra shoes and toiletries, even his suitcases. Before he leaves European Hospital, there is one last thing to give away. He goes down the stairs and past a hallway to the transfusion center, and donates his blood.

I can't sleep. Mahmoud is about to leave for Rafah, his backpack ready to go. European Hospital is just ten minutes away from the border crossing, and it is a fast route because the road through Rafah is empty. Mahmoud feels immense sadness at leaving his colleagues and little hope that the siege will end soon. He believes Israel's end goal is to destroy all the hospitals and leave no safe place at all, no infrastructure to allow anyone to keep living. As for the people who do return to their destroyed homes to try and rebuild, he worries they will simply become target practice for the IDF.

I ask Mahmoud what he has done with all this human suffering, all this heartbreak he has witnessed over the last week.

"I just can't do anything but keep going."

Mahmoud's trip to Gaza began with a death here in Dallas and concludes with another. I hadn't wanted to tell him while he was away, but he learns through his residency WhatsApp group that Dr. Amer Shakil, his former residency program director and a local humanitarian, has died from cancer.

"Do you think Dr. Shakil's *janaza* will be held before I get back?" Mahmoud asks. I think it will be the day after tomorrow, which is when Mahmoud's scheduled return flight arrives. But Mahmoud is still ten minutes away from the line in the sand that allows me to truly feel comfortable anticipating that he'll return. "Inshallah, you will be back in time," I text him.

At 2:15 a.m., I receive a photo of Mahmoud's passport with an exit stamp from The State of Palestine on 04-03-24, and then a few minutes later, "We crossed into Egypt."

My shoulders drop a weight they've been carrying since March 25, and it feels like I am breathing more deeply than I have since he left. "Alhamdulillah. Alhamdulillah. Oh alhamdulillah." I make *sujud* and cry from relief.

Mahmoud is relieved too, but on the bus drive back to Cairo, he starts to feel something he didn't when he left, a semblance of what I felt at his departure, a worry he hadn't experienced until now. He is worried for Omar.

Day 12: Wednesday, April 3

Mahmoud and I text back and forth as he approaches Cairo.

"I want to hear your stories, too," he tells me. He asks how it went with the kids, if I had help. "Sorry," he says, preemptively worried that I did not. "It must have been hard to be a solo parent for so long."

"Why are you sorry? I had a whole neighborhood and friend circle taking care of me. Allah has given me so much," I say. "Maybe that was an answer to your *duas*. Or my mother's."

And I mean it. So many friends and neighbors dropped by with food, or sent food, or checked in, and so many others I will likely never know made *dua* for us. It's not lost on me what a blessing that is. It took a village to enable Mahmoud to go and me to stay.

"Look at this headline," I text Mahmoud. "A Palestinian American doctor who volunteered at Nasser Hospital walked out of the White House. Just walked right out on Joe Biden during the meeting."

"I literally just read that. It is weird having internet connection," Mahmoud says. "I don't know him. I think his name is Thaer?"

Another thought pops into my head. "Hey Mahmoud. What's the first thing you want to do when you get back?"

"Tell you how grateful I am for you," he writes. "I really appreciate you being so supportive. I hope you know that I will never forget this. I can't thank you enough."

Day 13: Thursday, April 4

Our household's desperate wait for Mahmoud's return is apparent in our increasingly empty fridge, my car's diminishing gas range, and the constantly tripping circuit breaker of the upstairs loft, where I've been encamped. The supply of chai that Mahmoud had brewed and filled in mason jars for me has long since been depleted.

Domestic labor has been a source of constant negotiation between Mahmoud and me since having kids, and while I've often felt like I carry the heavier share of it, his time in Gaza has made the load he has been carrying much more visible to me.

I want to plan a whole reunion, where I pull Maymuna out of Montessori early and bring her and Qasim to the airport, where we have a sign and balloons as we wait in international arrivals for our most cherished Baba. The impracticalities of carrying a screaming baby with reflux and chasing a toddler around the airport take over, though, and Mahmoud lands earlier than I expected while I'm in the middle of a work meeting that I can't step out of. I end up arriving empty-handed to Mahmoud, who has passed border control and is already waiting patiently outside the airport.

I don't think I've ever been happier to see him, not on our *nikkah*, nor when I arrived in San Diego at the start of the pandemic to begin living with him while he was completing his fellowship. We say nothing, only hug for as long as I can remember we've hugged—maybe seven or ten six-second hugs all in one. I don't count and I don't let go.

When we get home, I ask Mahmoud how things are different. He tells me the first thing he noticed was the vibrant green of Dallas's spring, swaths and swaths of it on the drive home from the airport. He is much more aware of things that we so easily take for granted: the refrigerator that I thought was nearing empty has fruit, even if it's not the freshest; Qasim is sleeping in a crib rather than needing the comfort of someone's arms to feel safe. There are no fridges in the tents people are staying in in Gaza. There are no cribs. Seeing my world with his eyes now, I look at our master-bedroom suite and feel embarrassed at the excess of space for just two people.

Mahmoud is right back at the mosque for Isha that same night, hoping to spend the last vestiges of Ramadan in congregation. His medical school roommate, and one of his dearest friends, drives thirty minutes to be at Valley Ranch Islamic Center to pray alongside him. After Isha, the imam gives a short *khatira* about the hadith of Hanzala:

> I met Abu Bakr. He said: "Who are you?" He [Hanzala] said: "Hanzala has become a hypocrite." Abu Bakr said: "Glory be to Allah, what are you saying?" Thereupon he said: "I say that when we are in the company of Allah's Messenger ﷺ we ponder over Hellfire and Paradise as if we are seeing them with our very eyes, and when we are away from Allah's Messenger ﷺ we attend to our wives, our children, our business; most of these things [pertaining

to the afterlife] slip out of our minds." Abu Bakr said: "By Allah, I also experience the same." So I and Abu Bakr went to Allah's Messenger ﷺ and said to him: "O Allah's Messenger, Hanzala has become a hypocrite." Thereupon Allah's Messenger ﷺ said: "What has happened to you?" I said: "O Allah's Messenger, when we are in your company, we are reminded of Hellfire and Paradise as if we are seeing them with our own eyes, but whenever we go away from you and attend to our wives, children, and business, much of these things go out of our minds." Thereupon Allah's Messenger ﷺ said: "By Him in Whose hand is my life, if your state of mind remained the same as it is in my presence and you were always busy in remembrance [of Allah], the angels would shake hands with you in your beds and in your paths. But, Hanzala, time should be devoted [to worldly affairs] and time [should be devoted to prayer and meditation]." He said this thrice. (*Sahih Muslim*, no. 2750a)

"This is how I feel," Mahmoud says, turning to his friend. He feels like a *munafiq*—a hypocrite—being so close to Allah and so connected with His creation, only to return "back to normal" at home. But he is also reassured by this hadith, because the Prophet's ﷺ wisdom crosses fourteen hundred years to gently assure Mahmoud that it's OK; you can devote some time to your family now.

Dr. Amer Shakil is laid to rest the following afternoon. Mahmoud goes to the *janaza* with Qasim.

He sees so many of his former residency colleagues and teachers. Those who know he went to Gaza ask him about it, shaking their heads, lamenting what he saw, grateful he stayed safe. "It must have been a harrowing experience," the department chair says. Mahmoud doesn't say aloud that *it's harrowing for them.*

The deaths he saw in Gaza sprang from a violent, unnatural, entirely man-made catastrophe. Only a few of the dead were buried in separate graves; others ended up in unmarked, mass graves. And then there were those whose bodies were too shredded to be buried in full, and were buried as parts in sacks or bundled shrouds. Still others were obliterated entirely.

It occurs to Mahmoud that even though Dr. Shakil is older than most of the dead he prayed over in Gaza, he is young. He died in his early sixties. This would have shocked him before, but now he has experienced *janaza* prayers as part of his daily routine, and this has cemented in his psyche the reality that death is the only certainty of life. He is grateful even for the dignity of dying in peace.

Part Three

Heedlessness starts to trickle back into our lives slowly, insidiously, in a way that we almost don't notice. It starts with a sectional. We had most of the furniture we needed from our old house when we moved into our new home at the start of the new year, except for a living room sectional. I'd been too sleep-deprived in those early months with Qasim to shop for one, but now he was sleeping better. Yet it felt strange to bring this up with Mahmoud after his return from Gaza; how do you go from tending kids shot with drones to shopping for a couch? It reminds me of something Motaz said when he left Palestine: His disbelief was not only at what was happening in Palestine, but how the world was carrying on with business as usual on the outside. And so I say nothing about furniture.

Bombs continue to fall over Gaza, but without listening to them in Mahmoud's daily voice notes, they seem quieter, less frequent, only heard on snippets of Instagram stories—an air strike... a filtered picture of someone's restaurant meal... a child shredded ... someone's video of a coral-pink sunset in Cancun.

With Mahmoud's trip to Gaza receding into the past, my ever-present reminder of Allah becomes even less present. I remember the home invasion, and my calling upon Allah while tied up with those wires; it's closeness to death that naturally prioritizes God, reorienting us in ways that the comfortably living cannot know.

The Quran uses the parable of a ship at sea to highlight this tendency we humans have to lose focus:

> He is the One who enables you to travel on land and at sea until, when you are aboard the boats, and they sail with those on board under a favorable wind, and they are pleased with it, there comes upon them a violent wind, and the wave comes upon them from every direction, and they think that they are surrounded from all sides. They pray to Allah, having faith in Him alone, and say, "If You deliver us from this, we shall be grateful indeed." But as soon as He rescues them, they transgress in the land unjustly. O humanity! Your transgression is only against your own souls. There is only brief enjoyment in this worldly life, then to Us is your return, and then We will inform you of what you used to do. (Quran 10:22–23)

Mahmoud tries to stay connected to Gaza and his colleagues there. He meets with a lawyer who is collecting testimony for the International Centre of Justice for Palestinians. He writes a recommendation letter for Khidr for a job with MSF. He learns from Abdelkarim that Raed survived—the plastic surgeon closed his amputation wound—and he has since been discharged from the hospital. He asks about the young boy who was shot with the Terminator-style quadcopter; the one who had arrived to them bleeding and with blankets covered in ash and dust and dirt. Khidr tells him that he, unfortunately, did not survive. Mahmoud still remembers his face; he didn't even have a beard yet.

Whether it's the sense of purpose he had while caring for the people of Gaza or the feeling that he's being pulled away from constant reminders of his Lord, Mahmoud begins to feel drawn back to the place where he felt Allah's presence most. He calculates the rest of his vacation leave to confirm that he can indeed return for another mission to Gaza.

In February, Abdullah had put Mahmoud in touch with the NGO taking him to Gaza, and Mahmoud learned that he could join their next mission in March. He asked for a few days to talk with me first; he was weighing whether to go then or wait for a ceasefire.

Mahmoud got in touch with his old friend, Mohamad Abdelfattah. Their lives had continued on similar trajectories after Team Intifada; they attended UC Irvine together, then moved to Grenada to attend St. George's for medical school. They finished their fellowships within a year of each other—Mahmoud in wound care and Mohamad in critical care—and got married a year apart. Mohamad's son's due date was the day after Maymuna's, and his second child was born just a few months ago—six weeks after Qasim.

Mahmoud told Mohamad he had the opportunity to go to Gaza, but he wasn't sure if he should go with Qasim not even being four months old. Mohamad said he was waiting for a ceasefire, and Mahmoud decided that perhaps he should too.

Some days later during the State of the Union address, President Biden laid out a plan for an "emergency pier" to bring aid into Gaza, insisting on this puzzling and expensive approach rather than demand that Israel allow entry of aid through the existing land routes. Mahmoud immediately understood the implications of this—there would be no ceasefire in the foreseeable future. If he were to wait for one to volunteer in Gaza, he would be waiting for a long, long time. So he called and told the group that he would join the mission in March.

Perhaps the wheels were turning for Mohamad the same way, because a week after the State of the Union address, he sent Mahmoud a screenshot of an email he had received from the Palestinian American Medical Association inquiring whether Mohamad would be willing to join their first mission since the start of the siege, slated for the end of April.

"I'm strongly thinking of going," Mohamad wrote.

"I leave next Saturday with a different group," Mahmoud wrote back.

"Amazing! *Bessalameh*, bro," Mohamad replied. "Proud of you."

"Send me this guy's number," Mahmoud wrote. "Maybe I can go with you," and he leaves it at that—not willing to write "instead," yet not wanting to write "too."

"Let's make it happen," Mohamad said, and he gave Mahmoud Dr. Majdi Hamarshi's contact.

Dr. Hamarshi was very kind on the phone. Mahmoud included me in the conversation, and Dr. Hamarshi said that he appreciated that I was joining their discussion because the families of the physicians needed to be 100% on board with their loved ones going. He reassured me that safety was their top priority, but, of course, anything could happen. PAMA had been taking physicians to Palestine on medical missions for years, though of course the circumstances on the ground were vastly different now.

"When is the mission?" Mahmoud asked.

"We will leave April 27," Dr. Hamarshi said. My birthday, but more importantly, it would be over a full month after the other mission's departure date. Mahmoud told Dr. Hamarshi that he had the opportunity to go sooner, in just a few weeks.

"There is no need to delay then," Dr. Hamarshi advised Mahmoud, referencing a well-known hadith about hastening to do good deeds. "If those days line up, you should go with the other NGO."

"Well," Mahmoud said, glancing in my direction. "What if I go on both missions?"

Dr. Hamarshi paused. "I will leave that for you to discuss with your family."

As soon as he hung up the phone, I turned on Mahmoud. "We don't even know if you'll come back from the first trip and you're already wanting to go on two?" I demanded, formulating in my mind a case to make on Why This Is A Very Bad Idea. "Why not just take it one trip at a time? You know, like one day at a time, but instead one trip into a war zone at a time."

"Look," Mahmoud said, sitting me down on our blue velvet couch next to him in a weak attempt at quelling my opposition. "If something falls through with the first one, which is very possible by the way, and then Dr. Hamarshi's trip becomes full, I won't get to go at all."

He had a valid point—that NGO's last trip did fall through—but it's a point I could easily counter. "OK, and what if it does go through?" Mahmoud looked at me blankly. "Then, you will have gone on that trip and also be on the list to go again with Dr. Hamarshi."

"It's not like I can't take my name off the second trip," Mahmoud said.

I glared at him above my glasses as I would if he were telling me that no, it was not him who left his socks by the sink where he just did *wudu*. I knew him too well to accept that. "Mahmoud, you and I both know that you wouldn't back out of the second trip."

It's Eid al-Fitr, and even though Maymuna refuses to wear the Pakistani clothes I got her, and I have to scramble to find an American dress in the morning rush before prayer, and every photo has either Maymuna throwing a tantrum or Qasim crying, I'm grateful to celebrate this holiday—our first as a family of four. "I'm not sure I've shored up enough emotional reserve to do this again," I tell Mahmoud on the drive home from the mosque after the Eid prayer service. He hasn't even been home for a week, and we are already talking about the possibility of him leaving again. It feels so nice to be together. It's selfish, but I want to celebrate my birthday together too. It's the day Mahmoud would be leaving for Cairo if he goes on this second mission.

"We'll celebrate it," Mahmoud says. "Don't worry."

"You mean we'll celebrate it, and then you'll go?" I ask.

"I mean, I don't think I'm going," he says.

It's hard for Mahmoud to articulate what it's been like for him since he's been back. It doesn't really feel like the first trip ended. It feels like he just hit pause to take care of family responsibilities. He told Khidr and Abdelkarim when he was leaving al-Aqsa Hospital that he would try to come back. But the guilt weighs heavy no matter what he decides. If he forsakes this opportunity to go again when he has the time off and has his name on a roster, it will feel like he's forsaking the people of Gaza. Dr. Hamarshi told him that there would be a wound care nurse named Monica from Oregon on this mission, and the two of them are slated to establish a wound care clinic attached to the hospital where they would train local staff.

Yet Mahmoud also sees how much he's needed at home. Maymuna looks happier. She's sleeping better. She's not crying out for Baba. She is changing every day—her language is developing, mannerisms she had and phrases she said before he left are no longer the ones she uses now. And Qasim can be so challenging at times, fussing about not being able to move, cranky after his short naps—he is just not as easy a baby as Maymuna was. Mahmoud doesn't have to ask me if it was hard while he was gone. He knows it was, and he feels guilty asking me to do it again, to take over his role as parent in order for him to return to Gaza.

It feels significantly harder to make the decision this second time around. His internal dialogue runs like a reel in his mind: *Did I do my part? Do I need to go again? Am I going for the right reasons—not for the "glory," not for my friend, but for Allah?*

Dr. Hamarshi has asked all the participants to fill out some paperwork to submit to the WHO, and Mahmoud keeps delaying completing it.

Mahmoud hands me a mug of hot chai, fresh off the stove. I taught him how to make chai some years back, and now the student has become the master. I breathe in the smell and taste the hints of cardamom in the first sip. I missed his tea while he was gone.

"I told Dr. Hamarshi I'm not going," Mahmoud says.

I choke on my chai. "What!?" I sputter through coughs, my eyes bulging. "Give me some water," I bark, looking for a place to set my mug down where Maymuna can't run into it. I'm as incredulous that Mahmoud took his name off this second mission as I was when he first suggested putting his name on it.

"See? You even need me to get water for you," Mahmoud says with a half-smile, filling a cup for me at the sink. "You can't do another two weeks without me."

I take a gulp of water and settle myself down. "What did you tell Hamarshi?" I ask.

"I just told him it's too hard on my family. He wasn't mad or anything," Mahmoud says, sitting down next to me. "*Khalas*, I fulfilled my responsibility in Gaza and now it's time to fulfill my responsibilities here," he says, in a way that sounds like he is trying to convince himself more than me.

He's not really meeting my eyes, and I can tell he doesn't feel good about this decision. "Well, I'm . . . surprised," I say.

Mahmoud looks at me. "I thought you'd be happy."

I sigh. "Mahmoud, I've never wanted to stand in your way when it comes to this. Or really, when it comes to anything that is right." I pause. "I think you should honor your commitments."

Mahmoud looks at me dumbfounded. "You want me to go again?"

I shake my head. "I don't want you to go, of course not. I never want you to go." I don't even want to say what I am about to say. "But you have the chance to, and you want to . . . so I think you should."

Apparently, that is all he needs to hear, because Mahmoud takes it and runs with it. "I should call Hamarshi right now," he says, getting up and grabbing his phone from the kitchen counter. "He sent out an email yesterday looking for someone to fill my spot."

Dr. Hamarshi picks up. No, no one has taken Mahmoud's place since he sent out the request. Yes, it's still open if he wants it. But is he sure? Because he is getting authorization for each individual from the WHO, and after that, no changes allowed. So he's sure? OK, so it is done.

I reach for my own phone and scan the news headlines: Israel delays Rafah offensive given Iran's recent missile attack. Alhamdulillah, I think. Maybe Iran's largely performative display had some deterrent value. Even the Biden administration is acknowledging that Israel invading Rafah would be disaster on top of disaster, calling it a "red line" that the US will not enable with further arms. A Rafah ground invasion can't happen; that has been the call of the world for months. Maybe it really won't happen then, I think. Maybe there will even be a ceasefire.

I look up from my phone and see Mahmoud; I can feel his relief from across the room. I am not yet anxious myself. Maybe because, much like being a second-time parent, I have a better sense of what to expect. Or maybe because I know my tendency to overthink, to want to know the future so I can decide things in the present, as if it's not deciding in the present that creates the future.

Mahmoud's mission entry is delayed by two days. It buys us more time to gather supplies. This time, we fill nine suitcases chock-full of all sorts of donations: medical supplies like Silvadene, Xeroform, MediHoney, lidocaine, wound-vacuum supplies, gauze, gloves, and scrubs, as well as life supplies like clothes, shoes, and desperately needed baby formula.

The delay also allows Mahmoud to spend my birthday with me. 33. I feel fortunate to be here. As of this year, I have lived more years since the home invasion than before it, and so more of my life feels like it's been lived on its second chance. Perhaps all of my life is chance—chance that I was born and raised where I was, instead of being born and raised and likely to die much younger than 33 in a place like Gaza.

I feel guilty splurging on one of my favorite restaurants for my birthday dinner; there's a dissonance to eating a fancy meal two days before Mahmoud leaves to be among people who are starving. There's a dissonance even having a birthday when five hundred babies in Gaza didn't even live to see one.

I believe in a Day of Judgment, and I wonder how I will be asked about this. Those who don't believe in God often ask why He allows terrible things to happen, but I wonder more about why we humans allow terrible things to happen. Seven billion of us and we can only watch as basic, universal principles are trampled upon.

The server brings out a slice of carrot cake. I indulge in the cream cheese frosting, linger over the taste of clove and allspice, but in between, I wonder who has been exploited for me to enjoy this.

Mahmoud was worried about compassion fatigue among our community if he were to go to Gaza a second time. He didn't want our friends and neighbors to feel like they had to worry about him or step in again while he was away. Like me, he holds embers of guilt when it comes to asking for help.

This time, Mahmoud asked his parents to come. They arrive a few days before he leaves for Gaza and plan to stay through the first half of his trip.

I grew up with a very different cultural mindset around in-laws than Mahmoud did, and I assume my mother-in-law finds some of my formality with her a bit stifling. Unlike me, she thinks of us without the hyphenated add-ons—I am a daughter to her, the same as her own. She immediately makes herself at home, which means the hearty aroma of Arab stews bubbling on the stove, and it also means the blaring sounds of Arabic news carrying up the stairs and into the kids' rooms at 10:00 p.m.

Despite my hesitation about how this time will go, we get into a rhythm. It feels somewhat like I'm living with my parents again. Mahmoud's mother is rolling out phyllo dough and spinach pastries in the kitchen. His father tinkers around at the stove, trying to fix one of the burners. When Maymuna gets home from school and Qasim's nanny leaves, Jiddo and Teta read the kids storybooks and teach Maymuna the Arabic alphabet. Despite the fact that it hurts her aging fingers, despite the fact that I bought bottled lemon juice from the store, Mahmoud's mother still squeezes the lemons by hand so that the tahini sauce has fresh juice. I wonder if her coming here—cooking for us, being with us—is her way of mothering him. Of saying to him "It's OK. Be where you need to be. We'll help take care of things here."

When it comes time to say goodbye, Mahmoud and his mother embrace. She doesn't cry while he is still there in the entryway; she waits till he's out the door, down the steps, and in our neighbor's car before she sits down in the living room chair and makes *dua*. Only then do her tears begin to flow. A part of me thinks her sacrifice is much more agonizing than mine, and her patience much more commendable. Mahmoud is my husband, but he is her son, and I wonder who Qasim will be. Will he be the man who goes into a war zone not once, but twice? And who will I be as a mother to an adult son? Will I accept his choices, or will my opposition be much more visceral?

Day 1: Monday, April 29

On the flight to Cairo, Mahmoud is trying to lean his head against the seat in front of him to nap, but it's a struggle made more complicated by the woman sitting next to him. With her patterned socks peeking underneath her blanket and an open bag of snacks on her lap, she looks as though she has managed to get quite comfortable. Her expression, however, indicates otherwise; she is staring intently at her screen, clutching her blanket tightly.

Mahmoud glances over at what she's watching. He can't recall the name of the movie—the one with Denzel Washington where his son needs a heart transplant. He knows I would know the name, but I'm not there to ask. The woman is visibly upset at the impending heart surgery, so averse to the potential view of blood and human insides that she fast forwards through the climax of the movie.

Mahmoud continues observing her as she scrolls for a different film, one presumably more benign. She starts another movie in which the opening title card sets the scene to be sixty-five million years ago and then, in vivid computer graphics, a fly is shown being eaten by a lizard, and then the lizard is eaten by a dinosaur. The woman huffs, distraught. She turns off the movie and settles deeper into the seat, pulling up her blanket and closing her eyes.

Mahmoud wonders whether she has seen any of the images coming out of Gaza. What do people like her—people who can't handle witnessing suffering even when it's fictional, even when it's natural—what do they think when they see what is going on in Gaza? Do they even know, or do they just change the channel?

When Mahmoud arrives in Cairo, he learns from Mohamad that Thaer Ahmad is there too—the doctor who made headlines for walking out on Joe Biden at the end of Mahmoud's first trip. I watched his news interviews after the meeting at the White House where, before leaving, he hand-delivered a letter from a little orphan girl in Rafah directly addressed to Biden, beseeching him to stop the siege. "I can't tell you about malnutrition and famine, over, you know, soup and salad," he said, criticizing the Biden administration for its lack of action in restraining Israel.

Mohamad has coordinated a time for the three of them to get together; he is eager to meet Thaer in person. Thaer was supposed to be going to Gaza for a second mission too, but this time he has been denied; if he enters Gaza again, he will likely not be able to exit. He is a US citizen, but of Palestinian ethnicity, which means that the Israeli government will not recognize him as anything else. Mahmoud suspects it's also because of the notoriety from his walkout. Israel doesn't want more bad press.

Mahmoud comes to learn that Thaer, too, was part of the Viva Palestina convoy that he and Mohamad joined in 2009. They find wonder in the fact that they have no recollection of meeting each other there and at the *qadr* of Allah—how paths cross and recross while we may be none the wiser.

Mahmoud again wishes I was there; I am the question-asker between us. He imagines what I would ask Thaer: "What did it feel like to walk out on the supposedly most powerful man in the world?" "Do you think that was why you were denied a second mission?"

Thaer also imparts upon them his thoughts around his advocacy. There is the first part of going to Gaza, of course, that of providing direct aid. But there's the second part too, the work that starts upon leaving Gaza—using the experience to work on changing policy in one's home country. They must, he tells them, always stay useful.

And that is what he is now. Despite not being able to go on his planned medical mission, Thaer does not allow his time in Cairo to be wasted. There is a six-year-old girl who has been evacuated from Gaza; an NGO has coordinated treatment for her in the US, but she requires medical transport. Thaer has found a different way to serve; he is flying with the little girl to Portland.

Mahmoud and Mohamad get to work immediately after dinner, hauling the medical supplies procured in Cairo to their convoy. Mahmoud also meets with Dr. Younis, an endocrinologist who recently left Gaza. Dr. Younis has arranged for multiple coolers of insulin and several suitcases of medication to go with Mahmoud and the convoy, to help with the work he no longer can do himself.

Dr. Younis is a British citizen, but up until the siege, his life was in Gaza. He had a home there, three cars, and a family. When the siege began, he had the opportunity to leave and go to the UK. But he couldn't leave his people. He was running a free clinic for children with Type 1 diabetes with donated medicine from Australia and KinderUSA. Eventually one of his cars was stolen and another bombed, and then his extended family was killed. He couldn't bear the thought of losing his children, so he left with his wife and children in January—but not to the UK. He decided to stay in Egypt to help get medical aid into Gaza.

Mahmoud expresses his sadness at Dr. Younis's story of having to leave his home, along with appreciation for the help he is providing so the foreign doctors have the necessary medical supplies to do their work. "But wait," Mahmoud can't help but wonder. "What happened to the third car?"

Dr. Younis smiles wistfully. "I hope it remains, so I can use it when I return to Gaza one day."

Day 2: Tuesday, April 30

Getting across the border is always the worst part. For me this is due to fear of the dangers of transit, though for Mahmoud it also stems from frustration; the inefficiencies in the process drive him crazy. PAMA alone has close to three hundred bags, and there is one older Egyptian lady to check them all. Unbelievable, Mahmoud thinks, as he watches her slowly unzip the first one and begin rifling through its contents.

While waiting for the bags to be screened, Mahmoud gets to know Monica Johnson, the wound care nurse from Oregon with whom he'll be working. Mahmoud is expecting some ties to the cause—perhaps she is married to a Palestinian, or maybe she has a Muslim brother-in-law, or perhaps her sibling took her to a protest—something to explain how she ended up in Gaza. But he is surprised to learn that just a few months ago, Monica actually had very little idea of what was happening there at all.

Back in November, she came across a circular seeking nurse volunteers for Gaza. She had always had a helping heart and had been wanting to go on a medical mission for some time; she had submitted her name to volunteer in Afghanistan once in 2003, but had never heard back. With little information about the geopolitics of the region, she put her name down as a volunteer for Gaza. Some months went by, and she got a response asking if she was still interested. That was when she learned more about how dire the situation was in Palestine. She was horrified by what she saw.

A few of her colleagues tried to discourage her from going, but she wanted to be where the need was greatest. Monica actually has Ukrainian roots, but Gaza was where she felt called to. So now she is here to offer her expertise in wound care while learning one or two Arabic words a day to get by.

Mahmoud also meets a fellow named Mohamed Tawfik, a retina doctor who comes from a family of ophthalmologists. Mahmoud is convinced he must be the only Egyptian to have ever entered Gaza on an Egyptian passport; Egyptians are typically not allowed to cross the Suez Canal. Dr. Tawfik has arranged to bring with him a portable retina machine—a €180,000 medical device that he refuses to have tossed into a pile of luggage for screening. He goes to find one of the border personnel, and as it turns out, the agent's mother was once treated by Dr. Tawfik's father. The security guard gives Dr. Tawfik his blessings and lets him pass.

Their bags are finally screened, and Mahmoud, Mohamad Abdelfattah, Monica, and the rest of their multinational PAMA team (physicians from Jordan and Australia are with them as well) board a bus and enter Gaza. The team takes a picture together in front of the red **I ♥ GAZA** sign at the Rafah border crossing, and as soon as they cross, some locals already recognize Mahmoud and welcome him back, making it feel like a homecoming.

The sounds of the bombs are immediate. Mahmoud sees that Mohamad is initially a bit shaken by them, and is surprised that he himself is not more so. Still, Mohamad fits right in, and Mahmoud is impressed at the ease with which he is able to strike up a conversation with anyone who passes by. They learn that these bombs in particular are destroying homes close to the border that, alhamdulillah, have already been evacuated. Few complain now about the Israeli army destroying homes as they once did. With whole bloodlines lost, an empty home crumbled feels almost insignificant, if not an outright blessing. It's hard for Mahmoud to imagine not complaining about his home and his memories being blown to pieces, but the desperation and suffering is so great that this where many Palestinians are now.

Meanwhile, Mahmoud and Mohamad's friends back home have created a text thread with them to receive updates about their mission. A friend of theirs, writes, "20 years ago you met for the first time playing football and making the tiniest stance for Palestine. Now He has chosen y'all to be heroes together, Allahu akbar! We are beyond blessed to be your friends, please make tons of *duas* while you do the Lord's work."

Mahmoud doesn't particularly like hearing the word hero to describe himself. He appreciates the sentiment, and he doesn't want to feign humility—after all, he himself felt that admiration for Abdullah Fateh when he went. Still, after coming to Gaza, Mahmoud sees it differently—those truly worthy of admiration are the unsung heroes like Dr. Nasir and Dr. Malek, the ones who ask for nothing from the people and ask only from God, the ones who refuse to leave, the *murabitun*. Mahmoud can only hope that he is counted among them.

The students have had enough. They take to their universities in protest, from the West Coast to the East Coast and outside the US. The encampments they've set up on their college campuses include Jewish students, Muslim students, and nonreligious students from all walks of life, united together as people of conscience.

Like so many student movements before it, the pro-Palestine protestors are met with disgruntlement by their school administrators, some of whom unleash upon them violent police forces. Images circulate of beaten and bloodied students and even tenured professors dragged to the ground. A young PhD student from the University of Chicago is interviewed by the local Fox News station, where he delivers an impromptu monologue about there being limits to following orders, and he asks what is that limit if not fifteen thousand children dead, or perhaps fifty thousand, or perhaps two hundred thousand, or perhaps one million. What will it take? The protests last for weeks, until the Columbia encampment is forcibly dismantled, just days after Mahmoud leaves. Others follow. Over three thousand students are arrested; our community fundraises for bail for the students at the University of Texas at Dallas.

Meanwhile, Maymuna and I read her latest book fixation, *The Tiger Who Came to Tea*—one that I will likely have memorized within a few days, substituting "daddy's beer" with "baba's chai" each time. And each time we get to the part after the tiger leaves and the daddy walks through the door with his top hat off, Maymuna says, "I'd like to see Baba."

Other mothers tell me these early years go by so fast; I'll blink and I'll miss it. But motherhood has also had a way of freezing me in the time that I am in, stretching it so that it often feels like the moment I am in now is how it's always been and how it'll always be—I've always had Maymuna and Qasim, and Maymuna has always been a verbally precocious toddler and Qasim always a chubby baby with a gummy smile. It's only when I look at old photos that I am taken back to other times that felt like forever too. I think back to Mahmoud's first trip and how even the structure of Maymuna's sentences has matured in these few weeks between his missions.

I look at Maymuna, in her blue pajamas with pink hearts, her curly hair damp from her nighttime bath, and I imagine who she might be as a college student. Will she be like the ones who sit in a tent to protest the displaced Palestinians in their own make-shift tents pulled together from worn sheets? Will she march in solidarity with the people who left their destroyed homes and trekked to "safe zones," only to be displaced to another "human-itarian zone," and then bombed there?

The students have so much to lose. They are being doxed, job offers are being rescinded, and degrees are no longer being conferred. I remember Mahmoud saying that the community elders who had advised changing the Team Intifada name wor-ried that, even in the age before social media, the players would end up on some blacklist somewhere. Yet what does any of that matter in a world that can accept tens of thousands of children being killed by AI-guided bombs?

Growing up after 9/11, we were conditioned to keep our heads down, not ruffle too many feathers, become engineers or doctors to join the safe and stable upper middle class, and blend in with the white majority—not in color, but in socioeconomic status. That way, the world's problems wouldn't go away, but they would at least no longer apply to us. I think of Maymuna and hope that she can shed this baggage, with dreams bigger than maintaining a status quo that prioritizes self-serving gain. The student pro-tests give me hope that perhaps, if not in our lifetime, the next generation will one day manifest their posters and chants of a free, free Palestine.

Day 3: Wednesday, May 1

Even though Mahmoud spent a night at European Hospital at the beginning and end of his first mission, he only briefly toured the main hospital; his accommodations were in an administrative office separate from the main hospital itself. There, the foreign volunteer staff were sleeping anywhere they could find. He once encountered a surgeon on a glass-top office desk. Mahmoud himself had found a couch with a fan on his last night there before departing Gaza, which felt like an impossible indulgence.

It is only while working there now that he understands how different it is from Shuhada al-Aqsa. European Hospital is farther south and is massive in comparison. It has borne the brunt of absorbing the displaced Gazans from every which way searching for a "safe zone" in a city that, despite what Israel alleges, simply hasn't had any.

European Hospital is overwhelmed with workers and beggars and little kids and students and doctors all jumbled into one mass on a scale so large that is near impossible to weave through. Mahmoud is constantly bumping shoulders with someone or at risk of trampling over someone else; requests for money or food or cigarettes come at him from every direction. His head spins just trying to move from one end of a hallway to another.

Mahmoud, Mohamad, Dr. Tawfik (the Egyptian ophthalmologist), an ICU nurse from America, Modhir (an ER doctor from Australia), Adam Hamawy (a US Army surgeon), a colorectal surgeon from Jordan, and a pediatric ICU doctor from Saudi

Arabia are all staying in a room the size of a call room meant for one. There are five mats arranged on the floor immediately next to one another—fewer mats than people sharing the room. There is a sixth mat lying perpendicular to the others for one lucky person who will not have to sleep next to anyone (or perhaps unlucky because they instead will sleep next to several pairs of feet). Between their shoes, backpacks, extra scrubs, chargers, and a coffee machine, the ground is completely covered, and the clutter is overwhelming.

Mahmoud is finding it tougher this time emotionally too. There are so many children at European Hospital—far more than he saw at al-Aqsa, almost all walking barefoot in the dirt. It's impossible not to see Maymuna and Qasim in them. He sends me a picture of the children playing in the Quran school nearby, one of them grinning in a little orange shirt and jeans, perched on a ride-on car—a picture of innocence. One of the little girls he encounters calls him "Baba," and the older girls around her laugh, telling her in Arabic, "That's not your baba!" Mahmoud wonders if her baba is alive.

Those around him tell him he looks very depressed. The fatigue of being away from his own kids feels like the last legs of a marathon, even though he's just started. How much longer to the finish line where he can see them again? However, once Khidr learns Mahmoud is back and goes down to European Hospital on a donkey cart to pay him a visit, Mahmoud is all smiles. It feels like meeting an old friend after years apart, and it soothes some of his burgeoning homesickness.

Day 4: Thursday, May 2

With the looming threat of the Rafah invasion, Dr. Hamarshi had insisted that the group stay together—no working with the WHO to join missions in other hospitals like al-Aqsa in central Gaza or Kamal Adwan Hospital in the north. But Mahmoud wonders if there is a way to. Surely, if Khidr can make the trek down, Mahmoud can find a way up. He has brought supplies especially for their NICU, and having worked there before, he knows it would be easier to hit the ground running and be useful immediately. He floats the idea to Mohamad. Mohamad's wife had insisted that the two stick together. Mohamad is willing to go with him. "Not now though," Mohamad says. "We just got here." After the weekend, they agree, Mahmoud will look into requesting a change with the WHO to go to al-Aqsa for the second half of the trip.

When Mahmoud arrived home from Gaza after the first mission, one of the things that stood out to him was the sheer amount of personal space he had. Privacy and quiet, even elbow room, had been a commodity in Gaza.

"I don't know how you would handle it," he said, laughing. He knows me. Knows my tendency to become overstimulated when Maymuna presses the flute button on her musical Mozart

Magic Cube over and over and over, while Qasim screeches in the background because he wants food or maybe he wants milk or maybe he needs a nap or maybe he just wants to be held. I didn't tell Mahmoud how sometimes while he was away, I would pop in my noise-canceling headphones just to take the edge off a little bit.

"And I don't know how you would handle this," I replied. He would probably never know solo parenting for two weeks straight because I just didn't foresee ever leaving my kids for that long unless I was dead.

It's an adjustment for me this time to have Mahmoud's family here; I have to recalibrate how I recharge. The French doors of my office, adjacent to the living room, don't provide enough separation during my workday, and I can't simply sit in the silence of the evenings—silence isn't to be had anymore, even after the kids are down.

And while I do indeed have more of an idea of what to expect the second time around, the kids aren't any easier. Even Qasim seems to be aware enough this time to be missing his baba; he's fussy and unable to verbalize why. I put him down for a nap and come downstairs to find that Maymuna managed to yank a paring knife from a cutting board left on the countertop. I'm able to get it out of her little hands before she hurts herself, and then Qasim starts shrieking from his crib, so I go back upstairs to try and get him to sleep again. No matter what, it is excruciatingly apparent that without Mahmoud, I am down a parent, and I am outnumbered, and I am tired.

It is hard to reconcile that two mothers can have such different existences across the globe. I, whose needs for food, shelter, and safety are met, who has not been stripped of agency and dignity, can sit on top of Maslow's pyramid assessing how to meet my need to recharge my batteries after a day of working and caring for my kids; while at the same time, but in a different place, there exists a mother who cannot, will not, must not separate from her children for even a second. In my existence, I want desperately for my baby to fall asleep, and in hers, she wants desperately to be spared the anguish of him not waking.

PAMA has been developing a wound care service at European Hospital, and the volume of patients Mahmoud is seeing is double what it was at al-Aqsa just over a month ago. The patients gathered at the entrance of the clinic resemble a line at an under-staffed post office, and Mahmoud works like a clerk taking a package, putting a sticker on it, sending it off. The patients are shuffled through quickly, wound after wound, managed by a rotating local staff of three nurses and the foreign volunteers: Mahmoud; Monica; Modhir, the ER doctor from Australia; and Dr. Omar, the Sudanese trauma surgeon from America.

The need is enormous, and Mahmoud's initial thoughts of returning to al-Aqsa Hospital fall by the wayside. Between the number of people who have been displaced to Rafah and the increased number of air strikes creating ever more injuries and surgeries that require post-op care, the sheer volume of casualties at European Hospital far exceeds what Mahmoud saw at Deir al-Balah. There is limited time at European Hospital to bond with the patients and staff the way he did at al-Aqsa, no time to even wonder about the stories of the people he is treating; the only focus is on their wounds. It is almost a kind of dehuman-ization, not like the one that led to this genocide, but like the one that can be common in medicine, where a patient is divorced from their story and becomes only their immediate ailment. And yet the patients do not complain. Perhaps that feeling of wanting to be seen as a person, known beyond an immediate ailment, perhaps that, too, is a privilege. It assumes that everything else is stable, that the world makes sense, that everyone everywhere follows a universal code of common humanity. When the violence of what's been inflicted upon Palestine is as incomprehensible as it has been, when Palestinians have been dehumanized to the degree that allows such a violence to be inflicted upon them, then even the laws of basic pleasantries cease, and the doctor-patient relationship is reduced to its essential function—improving by even the most marginal degree the chance of survival.

The amputations, in particular, worry Mahmoud. Many of them must be left open, the flesh exposed. It's not as simple as a broken leg cut off; these open amputations take days or sometimes weeks to close. The extensive trauma requiring the amputation makes closing them technically challenging, and sometimes there just isn't enough time—more crush injuries arrive before existing patients can be properly managed. Other times, they must be left open to keep an eye on what appears to be tissue that's already infected, and in a setting as crowded and resource-poor as European Hospital, infections often get worse, not better.

Mahmoud is taking care of a seventy-year-old gentleman with an amputation that isn't closing—the bone is right to the edge of the skin, and he needs to be taken back to surgery to shave the stump bone down a bit further. He tells the nurse to let the orthopedic surgeon know, trusting the handoff, or at least hoping to; there is no other system to relay the message. But these nonemergent cases get put on the back burner as new limbs need to be amputated. This is exactly how the downstream deaths happen. People not killed in an air strike or who do not die in a first surgery can survive all of that only to die later of sepsis.

Sometimes the local doctors ask the foreign doctors if they think a limb can be salvaged or if it needs amputation. The answer is apparent, yet still they ask. One volunteer surgeon mentioned this habit during Mahmoud's first mission, and Mahmoud remembers it now when they ask him. "They know they need to amputate," the surgeon had said. "But they'll ask you because it doesn't feel believable that this is the thousandth time they are making the decision to take someone's limb—because in what world is that normal? They ask to make sure they're not going insane—this limb is diseased, right? It must be amputated, right?" They're not the ones who are insane, it's the world they're in that has lost its way.

Day 5: Friday, May 3

In a typical setting, a wound vacuum helps to draw out fluid and keep a wound clean, reducing the chance of it becoming infected, and it is changed two or three times a week. It's Mahmoud's second case of a wound vacuum left on a patient for two weeks without anyone checking it, and granulation tissue has developed around it, embedding the sponge of the vacuum into the newly formed tissue itself. It's a horrible sight and a nidus for infection, so Mahmoud tugs the vacuum off the wound, ripping it off the patient's leg. He attempts debriding and excising the residual sponge, but after a half hour they run out of oxygen and conscious sedation, and Mahmoud gives up. He will need to debride what's left later when he can use only lidocaine for pain control instead of full sedation, and when there are not as many other patients waiting.

The local staff are often apologetic to the foreign doctors, as if expressing the embarrassment of hosts welcoming guests to an untidy home at an inopportune time. But it's not their fault chaos has descended upon them in this way; in an offensive where even hospitals are targets, health-care protocols fall apart all too easily. Within the behemoth that is European Hospital, essential handoffs from foreign aid workers to local physicians have been missed, and such is the harmful help that sometimes comes from these missions; foreign doctors come and do what they can for a few weeks, but when they leave, if local staff have had to evacuate or there is no one immediately taking over, the patients' suffering increases in those gaps.

Things are no longer streamlined here the way they were before the siege; there are no distinct hospital teams with their own patient lists, and with the haphazard way that aid has been getting in, supplies that are available one week are no longer available the next. Even the supply room has become a disorganized hodgepodge, a nonintuitive system that feels like a house in which only the septuagenarian matriarch knows in which obscure drawer to find a matchbox. It's made worse by the fact that a Palestinian mother and child have taken refuge in the supply closet, so Mahmoud feels like he is intruding into their space every time he needs to grab some gloves or hand sanitizer.

Mahmoud feels his patience wearing thin. He has his first argument in Arabic with a patient's nurse. He's angry. He's angry that he saw his elderly patient again with the compromised amputation site, same as it was last time, with no handoff to the orthopedist. He's angry at the lack of follow-up by the nurses here—the central lines that get left in and the A-lines that don't get flushed. The patients are crashing in the ICU because their pressors have run out. Their mouths are left dry and crusty from lack of oral care. Bed sores—wounds not from blast injuries, but from the obliteration of resources—are cropping up everywhere. He's angry at the local nurses for being so checked out, angry now even at the way they speak, with their listless drawls and blank expressions. And then he feels ashamed for being angry.

I'm not the one there, but I try being at a remove to keep perspective. None of us can imagine the level of burnout of working endless hours unpaid while your loved ones die around you, I remind him. We don't know their backstories, if this is the second or third or fourth conflict they've lived through. I sense that behind Mahmoud's frustration, though, is not anger at anyone at all, but a helplessness within himself, a deep demoralization that he is fighting for people to survive in a system that is rapidly dying.

Day 6: Saturday, May 4

"I'm sad all the time," Mahmoud tells me. "But I'm also busy."

He tells me about a lady under ketamine yesterday who was making *dua* the whole time. The subconscious truly comes forward in these sedated patients, making evident their closeness to Allah and their heart's deepest desires. In the case of this woman, she was calling out for her own Mahmoud—her son. She called on her other children to look after him: "Mahmoud is always following you." Mahmoud inquires about this other Mahmoud, and learns that it is her youngest son, whose legs have been blown off, leaving him unable to run after his siblings anymore.

"It's really hard to see the children like this," Mahmoud says. There are far more children in external fixators this time. He thinks of Yassin, a little boy whose legs were crushed from an air strike and who comes to the wound care clinic for his amputation stumps—one above the knee and one below the knee. Every time Mahmoud takes the dressings off to clean them, Yassin clutches his mother's scarf and pulls it to cover his face. He doesn't like to look; the raw, red ends where his legs once were scare him.

Even though the bombs are less frequent and Mahmoud only heard one drone last night, the suffering of the children is much worse. So many children are skin and bones, covered in dirt, with missing limbs. "Mohamad said he saw a kid with no arms at all and a right-below-the-knee amputation yesterday, just hopping around on his one foot," he writes.

La hawla wa la quwwata illa billah. There is nothing else I can say to that.

Not the mosque next to the hospital, but the second closest to it, was hit by a bomb blast earlier today. Though it felt different than previous bombs, Mahmoud braced himself for a mass casualty arrival at the hospital; only it didn't come. He later learned it was a flash bomb, creating noise and shrapnel and shockwaves, but, fortunately, the injuries were not quite so grave. Still, a scald burn on one child and a deep foot wound on a one-year-old baby will leave scars for the children to remember this day.

"How is Maymuna?" Mahmoud asks, after telling me all this—I suspect to change the subject.

"She's fine," I reply, also wanting to change to yet another subject, not wanting to exacerbate Mahmoud's depression. But we've agreed on honesty both ways, so I add, "The Montessori said she's been really quiet the last couple days. I think she just misses you."

Mahmoud worries about the scars he is leaving on Maymuna with his absence. And he is not alone—Mohamad tells him that his son has had more toddler aggression, screaming at his aunt who visited, sitting on the dining chair that Mohamad normally occupies, running after cars that resemble his father's and crying out, "Baba!" The guilt of being away is far worse this time, perhaps because Mahmoud feels so ineffective. Does he have anything to show if he is of limited help in Gaza and his absence is causing distress at home? He can treat the wounds, sure, but he can do nothing to stop them from happening.

The mosque across the street from the hospital makes the Maghrib *adhan*, but it has heeded the warning of the flash bomb at the mosque nearby. After the ritual statements of "Come to prayer" and "Come to salvation," it calls to the people an uncommon appeal: "Pray in your homes." The next morning, it remains closed.

Day 7: Sunday, May 5

There is an established understanding in Gaza that once you vacate your home, you won't return. Many of the Palestinians now living in Gaza were displaced from the rest of Palestine in 1948 during the Nakba. They have been refused the right of return. This is why so many in the north of Gaza refused to leave in the initial evacuation demanded by Israel soon after October 7—they knew this would not be a temporary displacement. The demand itself was inhumane—a twenty-four-hour notice for a million people to leave and pack themselves into an even smaller area in Rafah. The infrastructure in Rafah simply could not absorb such a displacement; European Hospital was only a microcosm of it. And now the threat looms of Israel initiating a ground invasion into the very area it had initially demanded residents evacuate to.

"Before you hear anything, FAJR Scientific evacuated. They got some texts from unknown numbers saying 'All NGOs should evacuate the hospital now,'" Mahmoud writes. "Our team triple verified with WHO and there is no such credible threat."

I receive Mahmoud's text about NGOs evacuating from European Hospital while at a women's banquet. I have been asked to speak about Mahmoud's first mission in Gaza, and the organizers don't know that Mahmoud is there again now. It's my turn to come to the podium, and I have ten minutes to relay what Mahmoud saw and what he and I felt during his first trip. I tell the attendees about what we learned from the Palestinians—how they imbued in us a modicum of their own *tawakkul*. I share with them some images of the patients and the destruction inflicted upon the city. I read to them the texts Mahmoud and I exchanged in the aftermath of the al-Aqsa Hospital air strike, and then the World Central Kitchen air strike. I talk about how my mother-in-law raised these two boys who went to Gaza—Mahmoud and Omar—and the organizer interrupts to ask that she stand so that the room may give her a round of applause. I can see her from the front of the room, cupping her head in her hands to hide her tears, and when I return to my seat, she whispers, "I love you," and I know in this moment that she and I really are family.

I learn from Mahmoud after the event that it's not just FAJR that evacuated, it's also MSF and MedGlobal. Someone was tipping them off that they needed to leave, and fast. Mohamad was with the FAJR team when they made the decision to evacuate to their safe house, and they offered to take him along with them. He didn't even consider leaving Mahmoud—like the split-second decision when Mahmoud dove off the bluff for Aatif, Mohamad refused to leave Mahmoud. He had promised at the beginning that they would stick together, and even when given the choice to go, he kept his word.

This is the nature of going through situations like these, that it deepens the ties that two people already share, like it has between me and my mother-in-law. Mohamad and Mahmoud continue looking out for each other in this way, honoring their decades-long bond.

Mohamad hits Mahmoud with a pillow to the face—once, twice, a third time. If they aren't evacuating, they best be useful, and Mahmoud isn't when he's dead asleep.

One of the older doctors looks over at Mohamad and raises an eyebrow. "You know him for a long time or something?"

The fourth time does it, and Mahmoud starts getting up. "I've known him for twenty years," Mohamad says in Arabic as he walks out the door, and Mahmoud stumbles out after him, rubbing his eyes.

They cross the hospital courtyard and go to the emergency room. The ER has become somewhat of a shared responsibility; all of the foreign doctors have been floating in there, more so since one of the PAMA doctors was walking by one morning and found a local doctor sitting on the curb, beleaguered, holding his head in his hands. The PAMA doctor asked him what was wrong, and he replied, his voice thick with fatigue: "There's no one else in there but me."

It is chaos—a mix of both mildly injured and dying patients and their family members. Mahmoud functions essentially as a triage nurse—this patient has a blown pupil and needs to be prepped for neurosurgery; that patient's eyes and nose are intact, but her face is otherwise disfigured, and she requires plastic surgery. He sees Dr. Tawfik working endlessly as usual, examining someone with penetrating shrapnel to the eyeball. He turns around and a young man is being rapidly wheeled in, chest tubes overflowing with blood—two liters and still going. He needs to be rushed to the OR for cardiothoracic surgery, but Mahmoud can't find the CT surgeon. He tries to call Dr. Omar; it's not connecting. He sends a message: "Can you come to the CCU? Chest tubes overflowing," but it's not going through either. He does, however, find a young kid, one of many who have been acting as errand boys for the doctors. "Go get the Sudanese man!" he tells the boy in Arabic. The boy takes off running to the doctors' dormitory.

Dr. Omar, one of the PAMA doctors from America, is a trauma surgeon. By the time he scrubs in, the local CT surgeon has just arrived too; he received word about this case and has raced in, driving rapidly in a manner that can get one bombed. They get started. The anesthesiologist wants to keep the patient flat, but the CT surgeon disagrees; he should be on his side; it's a question of what will lend the best access to the chest. Dr. Omar steps in; there is no time for back-and-forth. *Malish*, let's defer to the CT surgeon and open his chest. They work rapidly, suctioning the blood, clamping the vessels. They've run out of blood to give him. As Dr. Omar attempts internal cardiac massage, the CT surgeon sees two devastating holes in the young man's heart.

They don't need to say anything further. Despite how often death has come, the staff remain sensitized. The noise of the ER is gone and there is only silence in the operating room. The two surgeons exchange looks and a brief nod. The man is pronounced a *shahid.* Mahmoud reflexively looks for the clock to see the time of death: 9:01 p.m. But the verse about not thinking of the *shuhada* as dead, for with Allah is their provision, comes to his mind.

Mahmoud goes with the surgeons to inform the family. They are patient; one lady calls softly for Allah and leaves the room, but the others are simply silent. May Allah have mercy on him and give his family a beautiful patience, Mahmoud thinks. They have done all they could for him on this side. All that remains is their *dua.*

FAJR Scientific has returned to European Hospital. It turns out the texts sent to them were a rumor being spread by a random number—perhaps a fear tactic. Mahmoud doesn't remember rumors being quite so prevalent on his last trip, but this time they seem constant. Rumors and whispers hang heavy in the air, creating a palpable dread.

The threats aren't just from the Israelis. They're from within too. With the mass destruction, violence and criminal behavior have sprouted up between the Palestinians themselves; Mahmoud recently treated a gunshot wound sustained in a fight over some food rations. Some people have become addicted to opioids from blast injuries, and others to black-market cigarettes. Having created lawlessness and desperation, the Israelis can turn some Palestinians into spies for a paltry price. It's valuable for them to know the comings and goings of local doctors and administrators; killing them means further annihilating the intellectual infrastructure of Gaza. "Be careful of that guy," someone tells Mahmoud in passing, about a man he has spotted several times in the hospital hallways, a man he had noticed who seemed to stand a little too close, be around a little too often.

Ahead of a possible Rafah invasion, the people living in tents on the hospital grounds and within its hallways have started to evacuate. Busloads of refugees are being sent to four-by-four-meter tents farther up in Khan Younis. Khan Younis was previously declared a safe zone by Israel for evacuees from the north, then bombed and decimated at the Israelis' whim. The mass graves of Nasser Hospital were discovered in Khan Younis only a few weeks ago; several hundred bodies were exhumed, many of whom were executed while still attached to medical devices, and some who were buried alive. Now Khan Younis is once again said to be safe, while Rafah is endangered. Situated near Rafah, European Hospital is restricting its volume to only patients and one immediate relative. No one knows how long any of these arbitrarily divided zones will remain "safe." They ride an Israeli carousel of death.

It seems that the threats of a Rafah invasion are founded, so I am perplexed about why the aid workers aren't evacuating as well. But Mahmoud reassures me this is actually keeping them safer. For one, if there are spies within the hospital, they are being moved out with the evacuees. Secondly, a hospital of just staff and patients has no reason to be invaded. There can't be a justifiable excuse to raid European Hospital.

It's a completely naive statement, meant to assure me. We both know that they don't need a reason to invade, that there is nothing to keep European Hospital from being invaded like al-Shifa and Nasser before it. "I don't know, Mahmoud," I say. "It's not as though Israel has never acted unjustifiably before."

I tell him that they shut down Al Jazeera today. It's an alarming move against democracy and freedom of the press; the broadcast channel for Al Jazeera now displays only the message: "In accordance with the government's decision, Al Jazeera channel broadcasts were stopped in Israel." Israel has been killing journalists regularly, close to one hundred so far. Few have continued reporting, given the dangers, but Hind Khoudary is one of those who remain. Mahmoud and Mohamad have the honor of meeting her.

Nothing is spared; no one is spared. Israel has killed doctors, journalists, and foreign aid workers. They have bombed hospitals, schools, and refugee camps. There is no such thing as a safe zone, no such thing as safe from Israel.

Day 8: Monday, May 6

"There are a lot of rumors about an attack soon, even in this hospital," Mahmoud sends me a message at four in the morning. "I'm just letting you know we received no official news and it's quiet here. They are still evacuating patients' families to the tents."

Sometimes I am up because Qasim has woken me for his last feed, but sometimes it's because I sleep with one eye open, waiting for these messages. I read Mahmoud's text right away, but before I can respond, Mahmoud writes, "We are fine, alhamdulillah. Just in case you hear anything."

These days it feels like I have more information on the outside than Mahmoud does from within. I look at the news and find an article about the impending Rafah invasion. It is time.

> The Israeli army announced on Monday that it issued an evacuation order for residents in the eastern outskirts of Rafah in the southern Gaza Strip. The directive reportedly aims to prepare for an upcoming military operation in the area.

> According to the announcement, residents and displaced Palestinians in the al-Shoka municipality area, as well as neighborhoods like al-Salam, al-Jeneina, Tabbat Ziraa, and al-Byouk, are required to leave their homes immediately. They are instructed to head towards an "expanded humanitarian zone" located in al-Mawasi, a coastal area between Rafah and Khan Yunis.

Al-Mawasi is barren land—no electricity, no clean water, no infrastructure exists there. And when they say that they've "issued an order," what they mean is that they've dropped leaflets on the area with a map chopping up the city into sections and demanding people squeeze into smaller and smaller pieces of land as the Israelis play roulette over which ones they will bomb for now. And for now, European Hospital, and therefore Mahmoud, is on the other side of the street from the Israelis' designated kill zone.

By early morning it hits the mainstream news: Israel begins its Rafah ground invasion.

On some level, Mahmoud is not surprised. We knew this was a possibility before he left for this trip, and the recent rumors and evacuation orders all seemed to suggest it would happen. What does it matter that the world said that a Rafah invasion would be a humanitarian disaster and a completely indefensible military action? What does it matter that Biden said it was a "red line?" His word has been meaningless.

Mahmoud's main concern is what will happen to European Hospital's operations. Even though the hospital is right outside the bombardment zone, the locals are getting nervous that the hospital will be invaded—especially if the foreign aid workers are evacuated. They look to the doctors to protect them, not just medically, but as a shield from the IDF.

The seizure of the Rafah border also affects Yassin. Mahmoud is changing his dressings when Yassin says, "I was supposed to leave Gaza with my mother yesterday." He was accepted for treatment in the US through HEAL Palestine, a nonprofit organization that has been coordinating international medical care for wounded children in Gaza. Even though he has been accepted into the US, with the border now closed, he cannot leave Gaza. And it is an indefinite postponement. One that could make the difference between survival and martyrdom. There is nothing Mahmoud can say to make it any better. Yassin allows Mahmoud to carry him to his wheelchair—a task he's normally only allowed his mother to do—and Mahmoud kisses his head.

When Mahmoud arrives back at the dormitory after his last clinic patient, he finds PAMA leadership there holding an impromptu meeting on what the Rafah invasion means for the group—and what it means is that nobody really has any idea what it means. It may mean they have to evacuate to another area of Gaza or completely leave the Strip. It may mean they have to stay put. They will connect with the WHO to find out if they can leave as soon as possible and when the earliest possible could be, but first they ask what each person wants.

Mahmoud is asked first and he looks over at Mohamad to confirm. Mohamad points down to the ground and mouths, "Stay here?" Mahmoud nods in confirmation. "I would rather stay until our end date," Mahmoud tells the PAMA lead. Mohamad and Monica agree, as do some others, while some want to leave sooner, or at least give it more thought.

Hours later though, the PAMA leadership provides an update. The team is told that the WHO will be coordinating their evacuation in the next forty-eight hours, and to keep a go bag ready. The leadership has decided that the entire team will evacuate European Hospital, with no person left behind.

The commotion begins during the Maghrib *adhan*. Screaming, noise. But it doesn't carry the normal wails and alarm that they have become used to after an air strike. Are those . . . ? They sound like . . . celebrations?

Mahmoud is sitting on the balcony of the dormitory, and he looks down from the railing. A child races through the courtyard, followed by his mother, but they don't look scared. They look happy. More Gazans pour into the hospital's plaza, dancing and celebrating. "Allahu akbar!" they yell.

"Ceasefire?!!!" Mahmoud writes to me in disbelief. "We heard there is a ceasefire!" The news has traveled faster than a wildfire. People are lifting others atop their shoulders as if they were celebrating a wedding. "Hamas has agreed to a ceasefire!" they cry out jubilantly. Alhamdulillah, Mahmoud thinks. He races out to find Mohamad and share the good news if it hasn't already spread to him.

Mahmoud is so happy to be in Gaza during this moment. *Samaiya doesn't have to worry about me anymore*, he thinks. He imagines at some point in the future when the siege ends, he will always remember that he was in Gaza when the ceasefire happened. Mahmoud thinks about Khalid ibn Walid and Uthman ibn Talha and Amr ibn Aws, among the last of those who became Muslim before the Conquest of Mecca, and therefore the last of those to receive the reward for migrating to Medina. He is so grateful that he and Mohamad were able to go to Gaza and provide aid before the ceasefire, the last of those who did, and that perhaps having done so will make them among the *murabitun* and will weigh heavy on their scales on The Last Day. He wishes Abdullah, who had been one of the few brave ones to go to the north, was here too to celebrate among the Palestinians.

In the distance, Mahmoud hears some bombs and thinks, *This must be the last of it.*

The bombings persist, and come with greater force. Maybe they're using up their arsenal while they can, like a toddler raging just before a time-out, Mahmoud thinks to himself. Maybe in a few hours, or tomorrow, there will be an actual cessation of fire—Hamas agreed, after all.

Mahmoud finds Mohamad in the ER. Mohamad has just returned from the hospital courtyard where he too heard the celebrations and the shouts of *hudna!*—ceasefire! Children had clung to him yelling, "Come with us, we will finally go back to our homes in the north!" But he is taking care of a two-year-old who arrived with a brain injury sustained in the ongoing air strikes. It's the kind of injury that will kill her slowly. It will be a drawn-out death as her mother looks on and says in anguish, "I wish we could switch places." Mohamad strokes the little girl's hair.

Mahmoud thinks about this mother. He would give up his life for Maymuna and Qasim, but the devastating part is that against the speed of an air strike, the parents of Gaza do not even get the chance to sacrifice their own lives for their children.

How unfortunate is this last death, the one to happen just before the ceasefire. How awful it will be for her mother, knowing that the difference between survival and martyrdom for her sweet daughter was the thinnest of margins—that the little girl survived the siege for seven months, only to become a *shahid* in its last few hours. Mahmoud touches her toes—they look so much like Maymuna's.

What Mahmoud has not yet learned, but will soon, is that while Hamas did accept the ceasefire deal mediated by Egypt and Qatar, Israel's war cabinet unanimously rejected it, opting to continue its military operations in Rafah. There is no ceasefire, and the little girl is not the last to die.

Day 9: Tuesday, May 7

Like 9/11, like the home invasion, like becoming a parent, like the events that are the before-it and after-it moments, the Rafah invasion becomes the dividing line of Mahmoud's Gaza trip. That was when things changed.

"The drones and bombings are constant, and we can feel the shockwaves to the building," Mahmoud says. The celebrations of a ceasefire were short-lived; the hopes of the bombs stopping dwindled quickly and are now dead.

Mahmoud is fasting today. His purpose is twofold: he has two fasts left for Shawwal and today is the 28th day of the month, and consuming less preserves more of the limited food supply, especially now that the border has been destroyed.

I see video of the I ♥ GAZA sign, the one at the Rafah border that Mahmoud stood in front of just one week ago, smiling with his team members, being bulldozed by an Israeli tank. It is reported on NBC News as, "Israel seizes Rafah crossing and the best Met Gala looks: Morning Rundown." It occurs to me that Mahmoud is experiencing history right here in this moment. There is no way that any sane person will look at the Rafah invasion one hundred years from now, or any slice of what has occurred in Gaza, and not be appalled by it. "How could this happen?" they will ask in the same way we ask about the Holocaust today. "How did the world let this happen? How did the world ogle celebrities at the Met Gala during a genocide?"

"What's going on in your head and heart right now?" I ask Mahmoud.

"Just a lot of hatred in my heart. And helplessness," he responds. The team is getting increasingly ill. Monica needed IV fluids. Two others have a gastrointestinal bug. Mohamad worked through a fever all day yesterday. And outside, anyone on the main road from the hospital to the Rafah border crossing is being shot on sight by the Israeli army. Mahmoud thought he'd heard all the war sounds in Gaza already: bombs, drones, F-16s, but now he is beginning to hear gunshots as well.

"Make as much *dua* as you can," I remind Mahmoud. "There is no veil between the oppressed and Allah." I don't want to tell him I feel his helplessness too. That in an ordinary situation, I would still trust that humanitarian workers would not end up in the cross fire of two combatants, but this is not ordinary. There is no concept of reciprocity—there are not even two equal combatants. At best, Israel has decided that there are two classes of people: Israeli Jews and Arabs. And there is a clearly superior and clearly inferior class. At worst, there are not two groups of people at all. "We are fighting human animals and we act accordingly," Yoav Gallant, Israel's defense minister, said months ago. The superpower has declared that there are no rules of engagement anymore. Humanitarian workers, health-care personnel, and foreign volunteers have all been killed by Israel in unbelievable numbers. International law is irrelevant.

"Let's go, Lakers, let's go?" my mother-in-law says, wheeling her bag to the garage door.

I chuckle. "I will miss you," I tell her, and I mean it. I have grown used to having her here; even the nightly Arabic news has morphed from an intrusion into a reliable companion, keeping my house from feeling too quiet in the dark. I will miss the company, and the food, and simply, I will miss her.

"Are you sure you don't want me to delay my flight?" she asks me.

With the Rafah invasion, I've wondered the same. I am not the same. I am distracted at work, preoccupied with reading the news. While I had not intended to share much about Mahmoud's trip, after the border seizure and renewed attention on Rafah, our mosque and medical community learned that Mahmoud is in European Hospital nearby, and they are worried. I am providing updates where I can, but between work and a two-and-a-half-year-old and a six-month-old, I only have so much time and energy.

Yet I also feel, though I'm not sure why, that I need to do this next week on my own. "I'll be OK," I say.

"If you need me to come again, say the word," she says. "I will turn right back around." She has enjoyed spending time with Maymuna and Qasim; it's felt like reliving Mahmoud's childhood all over again.

"Thank you, Aunty," I tell her. "I am so glad you came."

I take the kids along with me to the airport so they can say bye to their grandmother. But when we stop, Maymuna doesn't realize we are dropping Teta off; she thinks we are picking Baba up. It didn't even occur to me that she would remember the airport and that this was where she last saw Mahmoud a week ago. After we arrive at the curbside drop-off, she yells desperately, "We get Baba! We get Baba!"

I feel terrible breaking her little heart. "I'm so sorry May-muna," I say, holding her and wiping her tears. "We still have seven more bedtimes." She cries and cries, and all I can think is, *I hope it isn't more than seven.*

I ask Mahmoud if he thinks he'll get out of this alive. He says he does. The WHO is saying that it's not safe enough at the border to leave, nor on the road to get there. It is safe—or at least safer—in the hospital, so that is where they will stay.

They get mixed messages on when they will evacuate or whether they will at all. They also don't know whether they *must* evacuate or whether they can choose not to, with the caveat that if they don't, neither PAMA nor the WHO will be able to help them. Thus far, the Rafah border crossing has been the main point of entry into and exit from Gaza for aid workers and volunteers. There is no established plan for how the team would exit otherwise. Still, what Mahmoud believes to be the most likely scenario is that they will be able to leave as planned on Monday, May 13, which is also the planned entry date for PAMA's next mission. I am hoping so, for Maymuna's sake.

"I had a weird dream," Mahmoud writes, "that an Israeli mes-saged me and was laughing at our situation and saying welcome to Israel."

I wonder how prescient the dream is. I imagine the IDF invad-ing European Hospital and taking Mahmoud prisoner. I imagine him in a cell somewhere with a prison guard laughing, and per-haps it is the guard who says to Mahmoud, "Welcome to Israel." This is what happened with Dr. Adnan al-Bursh, the head of the orthopedic surgery department at al-Shifa. He continued to treat patients until he was taken prisoner some months after the siege began, and he was kept in detention in the West Bank without charges until he died from torture in April.

Our friends and acquaintances—people from our mosque, fellow physicians in our community—start recommending their political contacts to me: someone's sister previously worked as a congressional aide, someone's brother has a contact at the US Ambassador's office. Some people pass along their media contacts. "We need to move forward at an extremely fast pace, in literally panic mode," a physician in one of our community text groups says.

I appreciate the growing momentum, but I also hesitate to be alarmist. After all, Mahmoud's mission end date isn't for another week, and he himself stated emphatically that he wouldn't want to leave before then—it would feel like abandonment. He remembers the conversation Dr. Nasir had with the group about his young daughter who didn't want to leave; he understands.

Where I struggle most is the hesitation of placing my Mahmoud above any other Mahmoud there. My Mahmoud is a father, a physician, someone who is loved by his community—just like the many other men in Palestine. But my Mahmoud has the privilege of being seen as a full human, and I have the privilege of believing it is far more likely he will come home than that he won't. The Palestinians don't have that. They are not humanized, unless they are the "good" kind—the ones who aren't Muslim, or who aren't resisting, or who aren't men, but "innocent" women and children—and even then, they are granted only nominal humanity.

There is a tension for me in capitalizing on Mahmoud being American and, at the same time, recognizing that when he is there in Gaza, he feels he's among his own. There is a selfishness in raising the alarm only now, when it most directly affects me. Perhaps if we had raised the alarm and been in panic mode for the last seventy-five years, the last six months wouldn't have happened.

Mahmoud and Mohamad keep track of each other's whereabouts at all times. In Gaza, however, their differences become evident in two ways. The first is that Mahmoud is a deep sleeper, whereas Mohamad easily wakes from the shaking of the bombs. The second is their viewpoints on the burgeoning media attention around the fact that there are US citizens caught up in the aftermath of Israel's seizure of the Rafah border.

Mohamad has been vocal at rallies and protests. He doesn't like to be in front of a microphone, but he feels it is necessary for them to keep talking about Gaza, keep it in the news, lest people forget. Mahmoud, though, is the kind of person who will certainly join a protest for Gaza, but is likely do a U-turn if asked to speak on camera.

When I ask Mahmoud how he is dealing with the uncertainty, the proximity of the invasion, the death, he tells me over an audio message that they are all trying to stay busy with the work of caring for patients. The aid workers are OK, but the patients are very afraid. They're afraid that the doctors will be given the order to evacuate and that they will be stuck there, left to be massacred by Israeli forces. The ones who have broken hips or who are too sick to move recall the decomposing bodies of the babies in the

NICU who were left there by the IDF after they raided al-Nasr Hospital. About halfway through his voice note, a bomb goes off.

I know Mahmoud doesn't want media attention, but it occurs to me that it could give the doctors a chance to share testimonies of what they are seeing and show that if their plight is this difficult, what about that of the Palestinians?

I send the voice note with the bomb to NPR, and I suggest to Mahmoud that he transcribe his testimony—of the worried patients, of the lack of resources for burn victims, of patients who survive surgeries only to die on the floor three days later—into an op-ed. At the very least, if there is a spotlight on them, they have a chance to shine it onto Gaza and highlight the Rafah invasion—the operation that was said to be a "red line" but that has now come to pass, further exacerbating this horrifying humanitarian catastrophe.

Day 10: Wednesday, May 8

Mahmoud is spending some of his time in the ER, in addition to the wound care clinic, which has been seeing fewer patients since the invasion. The ER is not where he shines most as a doctor, but it is often all hands on deck, and he is helping care for some of the less critical patients and stabilizing others before they go to the OR. Today he is tending to a burn, several shrapnel injuries, a tense abdomen. The burn patient is only twelve years old. Mahmoud asks to speak to a family member to explain how to use Silvadene and gauze for wound care, but the child says he is by himself. Mahmoud has seen this, of course—WCNSFs, lone survivors of air strikes, little kids who are not just orphaned but who have, quite literally, no extended family left—but it always distresses him to see such a patient in front of him. "You are 100% alone?" Mahmoud asks. The boy nods his head, saying he lives in one of the tents across the street. Mahmoud gives him the wound care supplies and explains how to use them, and he takes off.

Another patient's X-ray shows shrapnel clearly stuck deep inside his forearm, and Mahmoud needs to cut through some skin to get to it. He asks the man if that's OK, but the man declines; he really must leave now, he says, because his two children are waiting to be buried.

A mass casualty arrives at the ER, and Mahmoud tends to a patient who looks to be losing a lot of blood from his leg. Mahmoud ties a tourniquet above the wound to slow it, but it's still flowing, and quickly. Adam Hamawy, the army surgeon, catches a look on his way to care for the eleven-year-old sister of his four-year-old patient who just died. "You can go tighter on that," he tells Mahmoud. "It needs to be painfully tight, and then tighter." Mahmoud tightens the tourniquet further, digging it into the man's leg as much as he can. The man needs surgery, but the local surgeon is overwhelmed, and all five operating rooms are full. Mahmoud sees this often, where all the needs are so dire that the prioritization of care leads to unfortunate and avoidable outcomes. The man is not slated to go to the OR for another thirty minutes, so Mahmoud packs the wound with some Surgicel he brought with him. It won't do much, but it's worth a try while he waits.

PAMA holds regular meetings to provide updates on the status of their exit, though they usually conclude that there is no update. They are hopeful that they will leave as scheduled on May 13, but if the WHO is able to coordinate a safe passage for them before then, they will certainly take it. European Hospital is technically in the "safe zone" because it is on the other side of the street from the zone the IDF is currently bombing, and the WHO is saying that it is still more dangerous to move the team through Rafah than to stay put.

Kurdi, Mohamad's best friend from all the way back in the Team Intifada days who traveled with him on the Viva Palestina convoy, is now a lawyer. Kurdi's friend Dina has been reaching out to her journalist contacts about Mahmoud and Mohamad. Media requests have started coming in—not from American ones yet, but from international outlets like TRT World and

AJ+. They want to know what the doctors are seeing in Gaza, what the situation is near Rafah, and how things have changed since the invasion.

Mahmoud's brother Omar sends me an article from *The Orange County Register*. It's primarily about his trip to Gaza last month, until the very end where Omar is quoted about Mahmoud being there now. But it's the title that gets me: "Medics from Southern California Stuck in Gaza Following Seizure of Eastern Rafah Border Crossing."

I get stuck on the word stuck. They're not stuck, right?

I send it to Mahmoud. "Mahmoud, would you say you're stuck?"

I call Donya, Mohamad's wife. "What do you think of this headline? It says they're stuck."

She gets my point. "Yeah, I mean they're not stuck, right? Like if they are able to leave by the 13th, then the news will have been blown out of proportion for no reason."

"Yeah, no, they're not stuck. I don't know." I pause. "Are we just in denial?" I ask Donya.

"Let's call Kurdi," she says.

Kurdi thinks I'm splitting hairs. "Well . . . they're stuck by elimination, right? There's no exit out."

"Yes, but they weren't slated to exit now anyway," I say.

Kurdi could say that I'm being overly precise, or he could say that I need to face the music. But instead he says, "Why don't we just say that we are hoping they don't become stuck. Their exit seems uncertain."

"Yes, yes. This I can agree with."

Only it doesn't really matter what I do and don't agree with, because a text goes out in our local eight-hundred-person physician group announcing that Mahmoud is indeed stuck in Gaza, and much like a stack of papers blown into the wind, it becomes impossible to contain.

"I wouldn't personally use the word stuck," I try anyway, "unless Mahmoud is not able to leave on the 13th." I tell them that I maintain that sufficient for us is Allah, and He is the best Disposer of Affairs. No one life is more worthy than another. There are hundreds of thousands of men in Gaza whose predicament has been, and likely will continue to be, far worse than that of Mahmoud. If a border reopens, Mahmoud can leave, but the others are truly stuck.

Mahmoud himself steps in from Gaza to share his thoughts too. "The word stuck doesn't sit well with me," he says. Of course he misses his family. Of course he intends to see his mission through and then come home. But until then, he says, "I'm honored to be here."

I try to respond to the onslaught of messages I start to get voicing concern for Mahmoud as the Rafah invasion continues. I tell my friends that we had these discussions before Mahmoud left the first time, and remind them that while he was there, the al-Aqsa air strike happened near his hospital, followed by the World Central Kitchen air strike. We never expected his missions in Gaza to be easy or certain, I say to myself as well as them, and it is uncertain times that increase us in *tawakkul.*

Day 11: Thursday, May 9

The American media has started covering the Rafah invasion in greater detail, and they've reached out to the doctors in Gaza for firsthand accounts. Mahmoud has been so preoccupied with the interviews that he hasn't been reciting as much Quran as he had been. He is thinking now about the *dua* the Prophet ﷺ made the night before the Battle of Badr. The Prophet ﷺ stayed up all night praying while his companions were asleep, and he continued until just before the battle: "O Allah, grant me what You have promised me, O Allah, give me what You have promised me. O Allah, if this small band of Muslims perishes, You will not be worshipped on the earth" (*Sahih Muslim*, no. 1763).

Badr is an underdog story—some three hundred early Muslims with just two horses against an army of over one thousand powerful Quraysh. It is also a lesson in *tawakkul*. No matter how dire the situation seems, certainty is found with Allah, not with us. It is He whom we rely upon.

The media, the politicians—they will do what they can. And Israel will do what it can. But what will come to pass is what Allah has decreed: *Qaddara Allahu wa ma sha'a fa'al.* A Palestinian child once said, "The rockets might be above us, but they've forgotten that Allah is above them." The bombings this morning as Israel expands its operations in Rafah are the most sustained and loudest Mahmoud has heard in all his time in Gaza. The walls of the hospital shake throughout Fajr. This is the time *dua* is needed the most.

Later that morning, Mahmoud is walking from the dormitory to the hospital when he sees a woman near the ER entrance wearing a full-length prayer *khimar*. The women of Gaza have taken to wearing their prayer garments inside and outside their homes—or tents—in case they are killed, so that even in death they may adhere to their modesty. She cries out, *"Abu Ali mat."* The father of Ali is dead. A handful of women reach her before she falls to the dirt in grief. They struggle to gather her to her feet. Mahmoud and another man walking by assist in carrying her to her tent. The heat outside is oppressive, but within these suffocating tents it is tenfold.

When Mahmoud arrives at the hospital, he finds it eerily quiet. Normally after bombings like those he heard in the morning, the ER would be full. But with the roads being blocked, few patients are able to make it to the hospital. Even hospital-to-hospital transfers are not allowed, so the flow of patients they had been receiving from the Kuwaiti Hospital has also come to a stop. Mahmoud wonders about those who are injured in the incessant bombing—what are they doing? Are they simply staying put, accepting that all roads lead to death anyway?

He makes his way to the ICU, where he is asked to consult on a patient requiring wound debridement in the OR. The patient is blind and paraplegic, and today Mahmoud also discovers maggots in his airway. Further care for him is futile in these conditions, and Mahmoud agrees with transitioning him to palliative care.

It's been difficult to make a case to the families to withdraw care for their loved ones. Yesterday Mahmoud and Modhir, the doctor from Australia, had a young patient who was paralyzed, had suffered brain damage, and who had festering wounds. The two explained to the boy's father that he would likely pass soon, and that the wound care team should primarily provide comfort measures—there was no use doing dressing changes now, as they would only worsen his pain.

Modhir shared his thoughts with Mahmoud. "It is not *wajib* to treat an illness," he said. "One can seek nontreatment as an option." He talked about the hadith of a woman with epilepsy who beseeched the Prophet ﷺ to cure her, but he ﷺ asked her if she desired to be cured or to endure with patience and be rewarded with Janna, and she chose the latter. He also mentioned the hadith of Musa (Moses) (*alayhi al-salam*) at his death:

> The angel of death was sent to Musa and when he went to him, Musa slapped him severely, spoiling one of his eyes. The angel went back to his Lord and said, "You sent me to a slave who does not want to die." Allah restored his eye and said, "Go back and tell him [Musa] to place his hand over the back of an ox, for he will be allowed to live for a number of years equal to the number of hairs coming under his hand." [So the angel came to him and told him the same.] Then Musa asked, "O my Lord! What will be then?" He said, "Death will be then." He said, "[Let it be] now." He asked Allah that He bring him near the Sacred Land at a distance of a stone's throw. Allah's Messenger ﷺ said, "Were I there I would show you the grave of Musa by the way near the red sand hill." (*Sahih Muslim*, no. 2372)

Sometimes the more merciful thing is to die. What's another few ox hairs, when they only prolong death?

Meanwhile outside the hospital, the cycles turn. A baby is born, and he and his mother are discharged two hours later. The mother names him Amir. The team takes a photo with the two, and Mahmoud smiles at the baby boy and says, "He is our Amir"—our prince. Mahmoud also learns of a baby boy who was born to a journalist living in a tent next to the emergency room of the hospital. It is his first son, born at the start of the siege. Everything his parents had prepared for him went unused as they were displaced again and again. At one point, the journalist was separated from his family for three months when they evacuated farther south and he stayed in the north to continue reporting. They have since reunited here outside European Hospital, but are facing another displacement with the Rafah invasion pushing people toward al-Mawasi.

This is the Israeli strategy—to make life untenable for the Palestinians. Even if they don't kill them directly, if they can strip life of all its essentials and make it unlivable, they will accomplish the same—more land free of Arabs. Shuffle them from one place to another so that there's no stability. Restrict access to fresh water so that all the water from the tap is salty. Starve them outright, or limit the food that can enter to just above 2,279 calories per person, which is the WHO recommendation. And now raze the border so that whatever little was getting in can be eliminated entirely.

The plates of falafel Mahmoud receives have gotten smaller. The six falafel that used to be dinner for one has become dinner for three. The patients have even less. Mahmoud treats a young girl who is with her aunt because her parents and siblings have all been killed. Mahmoud asks her aunt to make sure the little girl gets some nutrition, otherwise it will be hard for her wounds to heal. Her aunt says she doesn't have food for her, and the hospital is not giving any out. Mahmoud asks the pharmacy to dispense some Ensure to her, at the very least. When he returns to his dormitory, it feels painful to eat. He asks Modhir if he can take some of the falafel allotted to the doctors and give it to his patient. "*Tafaddal,*" he tells Mahmoud. Here you go.

Day 12: Friday, May 10

"The morale is low here," Mahmoud writes.

I imagine the fatigue I would hear in his voice if I could speak to him. Thus far, during both trips, Mahmoud has remained in a good headspace, which has been a source of reassurance for me. He has remained optimistic about the mission, the patients, and the return home. Hearing this admission feels unnerving—and foreboding.

I ask him to say more.

"It's just so hot. There's a sandstorm. The bombing is constant and heavy, and there are no patients to help because the roads are blocked. At night it's so cold." When patients do get brought in, they are often already dead—a woman with no face left, a man hemorrhaging into his chest. The listlessness is the worst. The feeling starts to set in that with no new patients to care for and the frequent calls to either amputate or withdraw care, they have left their families and their homes to be of limited use here to anyone. I wonder if this is part of the Israeli strategy too—not only to beat the Palestinians down, but to toy with the aid workers too, to make them watch the horror they inflict while the doctors just across the street are helpless to intervene.

Mahmoud tells me he was sitting on the balcony after Jumua today when he spotted some children fighting outside the hospital dormitory. He went downstairs to break it up as one of their fathers arrived. The father yelled at the children, "Israelis

aren't fighting us enough, so now you are fighting each other?"
he growled as he dragged his son away.

"Have you heard from your friends at al-Aqsa?" I ask Mahmoud. I've never met them, never even spoken to them, but still I worry about Khidr and Abdelkarim.

"Khidr didn't get the MSF job :\ " Mahmoud writes. He was the one Mahmoud had written a letter of recommendation for. "Abdelkarim's mom made *mamoul* in anticipation of meeting me, but unfortunately it's not looking like I will see them." Al-Aqsa Hospital, where Khidr and Abdelkarim continue to work, is in even more dire conditions; they are looking at twenty-four hours of fuel left.

With the Rafah border destroyed, supplies are running critically low at European Hospital, too—not just the medications, but the essentials like soap, gloves, chucks, the bare minimum needed to serve the patients. Without skin, the body leaks tissue fluid; this is what happens to burn patients, and the absorbent pads keep them dry, which both lowers their risk of infection and keeps their temperature up. There aren't enough, and the patients, sick and burned, are shivering.

More of the refugees who have been staying in encampments by the hospital are slated to leave for al-Mawasi. Every day Mahmoud has waved hi and bye to children on his walks from the hospital to his dormitory and back. Today the children tell him they will miss him. "Every day the hospital looks more and more empty," Mahmoud says.

"I can't tell if that's a good thing or a bad thing," I say.

"Me neither," he writes back. I worry that Israel is herding all the refugees to the seashore in al-Mawasi, only to drop a massive bomb there and kill them all in one go.

More than I worry about Mahmoud, I simply miss his presence. "Even during your first trip, I have never wanted you home as much as I do now," I tell Mahmoud. "It's hard to describe. It's like hunger pangs, but in my heart. It's a pain in my heart. I wish I could give you wings and you could leave. You will come home on Monday, right?" I ask him, as if he can take a telescope and look into the future and tell me, *Yes, I'll be home, and I'll make chai and you'll make waffles and we'll be happy just to be next to each other having breakfast again.*

"Inshallah. We are hoping we can, yes," Mahmoud says. His friend from Miami is preparing for the next mission, which is slated to enter Gaza on May 13, the same day as Mahmoud's scheduled departure. "So that's a good sign," he says.

An hour later, Mahmoud is calling me. I answer the phone, but there is no connection. "I picked up," I text him. "Can you hear me?"

"We were in a meeting," I see his response, and then a voice note. I listen right away.

"No." I type to Mahmoud.

"No."

"No."

"No."

"No."

"No no no no."

I type it over and over again, as if by writing it a few more times, he can rewind what he said, erase it, unsay it.

I play his note over again. Perhaps I am wrong. I must be wrong. God, I am wrong! Please God, I am wrong! God, let me be wrong.

I listen again.

"Assalamu alaikum. So, on Monday they're going to take only two people. I'm sorry. They're going to take two people, and they're going to put in a third name just in case. They're going through a different crossing, Kerem, and if that goes well— they're calling it a 'trial crossing'—if it goes well, more crossings will be planned. We don't know when. We asked, but we don't know."

More texts come in:

"*Hasbi Allahu wa ni'mal wakil.*"

"I'm very sorry, honey."

I'm shaky, and I start to cry. It is 1:28 p.m., and I have a one-on-one meeting with one of my direct reports at 1:30.

In my medical school application essay, I wrote about my ability to compartmentalize all through high school. How I divided myself up after the home invasion: a part of me for processing that trauma and a part of me to hold onto my class ranking and see it through, to graduate valedictorian of my high school class. I compartmentalized a part of myself in residency to go through separating during my intern year, and finalizing my divorce between seventy-hour weeks on the psychiatry inpatient units and one of the busiest consult services in the US. I am used to living piecemeal like this, but today, two minutes before my one-on-one, I have reached the limits of what I can compartmentalize.

"My husband is not leaving Gaza," I let my boss know. I tell the rest of the team I have a family emergency and that I will not be back today, and may not be back Monday either. I am scared to say more, and I am hesitant to take more time off than this. People have lost their jobs for voicing their support for the civilians in Gaza, for protesting their slaughter. I do the calculus immediately: I need this job now more than I did two minutes ago. Two minutes ago, I still believed at my core that my husband would be returning as planned. Two minutes later I don't, and I realize the time really may be here that I must ready myself, emotionally and logistically, that he won't come home at all.

When I was young, my father once spent six weeks in Canada after being turned away at the US–Canada border following a business trip. There was some technicality about the address on his visa not being up to date.

This would likely have been a nonissue, except that it occurred six months after 9/11. People in the community—Pakistani adults my parents knew—were getting deported. A prominent charity based in Richardson was deemed a terrorist organization. And the FBI was spying on Muslims in mosques.

My dad's mistake—not filing a change of address—was the kind you didn't want to be making when Muslims were under so much scrutiny. Aside from sending my mother into a panic, there was ultimately little consequence. He eventually came home, and things returned to normal, except that my father would not keep a long beard for the next two decades.

This memory returns to me on Friday afternoon, a few hours after I learn about Mahmoud being stuck in Gaza. My sister

Sarah had planned to come by after work, and when she does, I tell her Mahmoud isn't coming home.

"I wonder if this is what Mom felt like when Pa was stuck in Canada," I say.

She looks at me with a mixture of sympathy and alarm. "I think this situation is a little more dire. Mahmoud is stuck in a war zone."

She is worried I am in denial. I'm not though. There are no planes nor trains out of Gaza. There is not even the same border crossing they used to enter. I know what this could mean, but my heart hurts too much to start planning for an unknown future. Maybe the delay will be a few days. Maybe it will be a few weeks. Maybe it will be the rest of this lifetime.

After the kids are down and Sarah leaves, I hear from Mahmoud again. "I'm dehydrated and my stomach hurts," he says.

I'm walking into our room sipping water from the Stanley cup he usually fills for me before bed. I feel immediate guilt. "What is the water situation?" I ask him.

"Not much. Me and Mohamad were sharing a bottle last night." He ate something bad last night, he tells me. He's not well. "So many bombs this morning. Just so many."

He is going to try to sleep off this GI bug. His stomach cramps are intense, and he is too dizzy to go to the hospital to look for water. Mohamad goes to look for him.

I can read the demoralization between the lines. Yet Mahmoud tries to comfort me. He reassures me he's coming home; he doesn't know when, but he'll come home inshallah.

I lie across our bed, as if breaching the invisible barrier that demarcates my side and his side brings me magically closer to him. I look on Instagram to see if there are updates that will tell me what will happen. Instead, I see posts about how beautiful the northern lights are tonight—bright pink and green. Mahmoud has been to Alaska, but I never have; we'd talked about going to see the northern lights together. I can't move; I can only cry. It's the closest I feel to the possibility, more than I ever did in al-Aqsa, that this is the time—this may really be the time—that Mahmoud will not survive.

Day 13: Saturday, May 11

I give myself Friday night to be near catatonic from grief, sadness, and anxiety. By Saturday morning, it's time to pull myself together. My children need me, and Mahmoud needs me. I have to mobilize. If Mahmoud has thus far largely driven the ship for going to Gaza, I need to take the helm for getting him out.

I first read Mahmoud's overnight messages: the drinking water ended up arriving four hours later—a whole liter. A bevy of messages have come in overnight from the California contingent working in PST—primarily Mohamad's wife Donya, his best friend Kurdi, and his friend Dina. Donya's eyes fall on the email that Mohamad sent her before leaving, with the subject "worst-case scenario." She doesn't open it. The scenario has not come to pass, and we are now banding together to keep it that way.

I have also been added to several other WhatsApp groups with lawyers, PR professionals, and political strategists. I'm not exactly sure who has started them nor who is leading them, but anyone from coast-to-coast who says "I've worked on The Hill for ten years" is looped in. I will come to learn over the next few days that a dozen-and-a-half people on our community WhatsApp groups know someone who knows someone "with a direct line to the State Department." I'm amazed at our community's resourcefulness. I am thrust into a world completely foreign to my healthcare world; it feels like being on an episode of *House of Cards* rather than *Scrubs*.

I am fumbling with my dinging phone to read the lightning-fast texts while breastfeeding Qasim, when Maymuna starts whining for breakfast and my mother rings the bell and my sister calls me—can I send a photo of Mahmoud right away for her to use for their phone-banking campaign? I unlatch Qasim to unlock the door so I don't keep my mother waiting, and while he starts wailing for more, Maymuna pulls at my pant leg asking for Cheerios. I finish nursing Qasim, fix breakfast for Maymuna, and make chai for my mom, while I get another fifty messages and four missed calls on my phone. I'm overstimulated and stretched thin and it's all too much. I send Qasim to my neighbor's house, and by the time he comes back, Maymuna is napping. When she wakes up, she goes to a different neighbor's house for the afternoon.

I realize quickly that I simply cannot sustain the pace I need to be operating at and solo parent two kids at the same time. If I am going to get through this time, I am going to have to keep doing that dreaded thing—ask for help. People know about Mahmoud, and they're messaging: "Let me know how I can help." So I decide to state my needs plainly and put together an Excel sheet for each day next week.

The 7–9 a.m. and 5–7 p.m. stretches of time with the kids are the hardest: breastfeeding Qasim, getting Maymuna ready for Montessori, making breakfast and setting Maymuna up with her food, strapping them both in the car, timing Maymuna's drop-off so I can get home before Qasim takes his first nap instead of him falling asleep in the car and then not transferring. I can ask to have breakfast taken off my plate—that should streamline the morning.

From 5–7 p.m. is trickier. I could use help with dinner, but what I really need is a second set of hands after the nanny goes home. I write down 5–6 p.m. and 6–7 p.m. shifts for people to sign up to just be here. Just hold the baby or play animals with Maymuna. They do so much better with someone new to sit down and play with instead of an overextended mother with a very short supply of attention remaining.

I don't have too much time to fixate on the discomfort of sending my neighbor the sheet. Time is scarce right now, after all, and I shoo away the voice in my head that says I'm *mangu*—needy. I know I will be a better mother to my children if I offload some of these physical needs; I just have to step over the albatross of shame and ask my friend, "Can you please coordinate this? This is how I could really use help this week."

My conversations with Mahmoud change. There's no time anymore to ask him how he is doing, if his cramps have resolved, if he still has water.

"I need the PAMA roster," I demand, and when he doesn't respond fast enough, I message Dr. Hamarshi.

"I need you to send me a voice note documenting the water situation," I tell Mahmoud.

"What's going on?" Mahmoud asks me.

"We're preparing talking points for the media."

Mahmoud used to joke when we'd get into arguments that I should have gone into public relations; I am relentlessly exacting about word choice and too incisive for my own good. I tell him he wished too hard, and that Amina, the wife of one of the doctors there, works with someone who has agreed to help us pro bono, and that we are already behind. As Kurdi has gently reprimanded us, we should have been pushing the media front days ago when we were, instead, quibbling over the meaning of the word "stuck." Dina, meanwhile, is working with a contact to get the doctors on Ayman Mohyeldin's show on MSNBC tomorrow night.

I pass on the photo of the team in front of the **I ♥ GAZA** sign, and someone in the group turns it into a social media flyer with a caption about the twenty American health-care workers trapped in Gaza. We go back and forth about hashtags, but we eventually choose #LetOurDocsGo, which captures the fact that the border closing hasn't just rendered our loved ones unable to leave Gaza, it has also kept aid from getting in. The doctors there now are quickly running out of the supplies they brought with them to be able to help. The next set of aid workers needs to get in just as much as Mahmoud and his team need to get out.

The caption is edited; the picture is done. Mahmoud is smiling there on the right, none the wiser in that photo taken just a few weeks ago that it would end up being spread all over Instagram.

Day 14: Sunday, May 12

Mahmoud wakes up on Sunday finally feeling like he is recovering from the GI bug that kept him asleep much of yesterday. He got a little arrogant and started thinking of himself as Ghazzawi, a local, but he isn't, and he got reminded of that in no uncertain terms.

All Mahmoud has been focused on since learning that he won't be leaving on Monday is how hard I must be taking it, how hard it will be for me to keep taking care of the kids while we wait, and the uncertainty of it all. If there were a definitive date, that would be one thing, but to just have no plan? He knows how much it drives me crazy when he doesn't have a plan.

But he isn't much worried about himself. When the group was first told they wouldn't be going home, Mahmoud learned a lot from Adam Hamawy's composure. Hamawy is the US Army surgeon on their team who has served in combat zones for years. His presence is calming, but not passive—he stays focused on work and doesn't get shaken by the uncertainty of their exit. "Whatever happens, happens," he says. "Nothing is certain. Things are fluid." He's learned from past experience not to tell his family when or how he may leave. He only tells them once he has.

Mahmoud is also skeptical of the media push that we have been coordinating. NPR has already contacted him for an interview tomorrow. Mohamad is pegged to be on *Ayman* on MSNBC tonight.

I try to convince him. "Everyone Stateside has been advising us to make as much noise as possible. That doing so will increase the pressure. I hope you understand."

He does, but he's not convinced this is the best or even the safest plan. He has always been the kind of person who shies away from the spotlight; whether it's from a childhood stutter, the fact that he can't stand the sound of his own voice, or simply anxiety about public speaking, he isn't sure.

It also feels risky to no longer be faceless and nameless. The more the doctors here talk about their situation, the more scrutiny they will have to endure, and the more the IDF is likely to mess with them. We think the deterrent effect of negative press would be useful in shaming Israel, but the Israeli government has no shame; in his estimation, a media firestorm won't move the needle in the least. Besides, PAMA leadership is already in contact with a WHO liaison, and he's been very communicative. The WHO is doing what it can.

Before I learned Mahmoud wasn't going to be coming home as scheduled, I had planned to meet my mother, Sarah, and her mother-in-law for Mother's Day brunch. It turns out I am doing very little celebrating today. Mahmoud's residency friend Maheen and her husband have insisted on taking me in.

I get the kids ready in the morning, but Maymuna resists. "I want spider shirt," she wails, and it's early enough in the morning that my empathy outweighs my irritation. But I can't fix this; I don't know what the spider shirt is. "Which one is the spider shirt, mama?" I ask her, a very unreasonable request for a

176

two-year-old making it clear through her tantrum that the only way she can describe it is the spider shirt. I know she has no spider shirts, I know she means something other than what she's saying, and we are at an impasse. I can only hold her, rock her, and say, "Maymuna, I know how hard it is to want something and not have it."

She cries as I load her into the car followed by Qasim, who by now is himself cranky and overtired, and I make the drive to Maheen and her husband's home, where their nanny takes the kids. My friends feed me breakfast and send me up to the office where I spend the next hours attending a family meeting with PAMA; answering a phone call from an NPR reporter; and then being patched into a conference call with Amina, who has just returned from her father's funeral, and a lawyer from UCLA, who is giving me completely opposite advice from the political and media people yesterday.

"It has only been a few days. You need to give time for silent diplomacy," he says knowingly. He starts naming senators he believes will be sympathetic to the cause of twenty American aid workers stuck in Gaza, names I have to Google while on the call because I am so politically out of touch. "I have a meeting with Senator Van Hollen on Thursday," he reassures us.

"We are thinking they will still be there on Thursday?" I ask, unable to contain my alarm at the prospect of this. I tell him that another lawyer has advised us to start talking to the media as soon as possible.

He tells us he totally disagrees. "Getting the media involved is just going to turn this into political football," he says. I open another Google tab to search "political football meaning."

I am at a loss, and I am overwhelmed, and then I remember the sister of an ambassador who reached out to me earlier in the week. There have been so many texts and so many people who know someone that I can't keep track of them all. But I remember receiving a message from her, and she is my next call.

She talks to me cryptically—there is little her brother can do; there was little he could do when she herself was once detained while volunteering as an aid worker in Bangladesh. However, her brother has said that the highest levels of government know about my husband and the other aid workers. That is all she can say, but she repeats the phrase "highest levels" enough for me to think Secretary Blinken—if not President Biden—might be following the circumstances of little old Mahmoud Sabha of Dallas, Texas, in Gaza. Whether they care, I don't know, but a part of me is relieved that they are aware. I still want to know one thing, though.

"What would you do if it were your husband?" I ask her. "Would you talk to the media?"

She doesn't even think about it. She uses no political jargon. She says plainly, "I would be as loud as possible."

Over lunch, Maheen, her husband, and I discuss the options. One is to let the political backchanneling quietly bring the doctors home. The other is to use the media to get the story out and put pressure on the powers that be for their safe return. The underlying question is whether having the doctors in the media puts a target on their back, or whether it raises their profile and keeps them safer. *It's a gamble on their life*, I think.

I want someone to tell me the right answer. I'm completely out of my wheelhouse. When the kids wake up, I scoop them up and we start driving home. I ponder the options some more. What if we made a mistake? I want to backtrack. I want to pull back from the media push we've already initiated—the *Ayman* show, NPR, and now CNN and ABC have contacted the doctors as well.

Just as I'm thinking that in these uncertain times, all I need is Allah, I get a text from Maheen. I have gotten entirely too side-tracked these past two days, thinking this one person has the answer or that one media story will make a difference.

"Samaiya, read the *istikhara dua* after each prayer," she writes. "Allah will guide you on the best approach."

Mahmoud spends the early part of the day visiting the UN school adjacent to the hospital grounds. Many of the kids that greet the staff every morning and evening live there, and while some have left for al-Mawasi, others have stayed put. He remembers being impressed with them when the PAMA team first arrived in Gaza and he would see them diligently studying their Quran. So many of them are *huffadh* already. The children put on a play recounting the death of one of the girls' fathers—even the sound effects feel real, until one of the children interrupts to announce a drone is overhead. At the end of the play, one of the children asks the martyrs to forgive those still living. Mahmoud wishes he could ask all of Gaza to forgive him.

Mahmoud lingers, sitting with the children a little longer. Some of the older children ask him his age, and they laugh when they find out he is nearing forty and has little kids; their grand-parents are in their forties, they say. One of the girls asks Mahmoud what his favorite food is, and she tells him about hers—it's *m'sakhan*. She was the one who lost her father. He wonders if she misses eating *m'sakhan* with him.

Back at the clinic, he greets Muhammad, a nurse who has a special *nur* (light) on his face—he is smiling as though he hasn't been living through a siege for the past seven months. Mahmoud learns that he used to work at al-Shifa Hospital before the Israelis destroyed it two months ago. Mahmoud asks Muhammad what it was like.

MSF and the Red Cross were told to evacuate the day before the invasion in March, Muhammad says, but he and the staff were not given any orders to do so, and so they were still there at the hospital when the Israelis raided. He tells Mahmoud about the tanks outside the hospital and the soldiers coming in. The soldiers asked workers about the hospital basement, where the storage was, insinuating that it was used for nefarious activities. Muhammad went down there often to get supplies and he knew that was all there was, but the truth did not matter. Everyone was ordered to leave—even the patients in their beds. Those who could walk, did, and others were pushed in their beds or in office chairs for thirty kilometers toward al-Mawasi. Between the distance and the time spent at checkpoints, the staff and patients walked for two days.

Mahmoud tries to imagine what it would be like for a hospital in the States to experience such a thing. These are the stories that need to be on CNN—not Mahmoud being unable to leave the hospital, but those who are forced to leave the hospital. Theirs are the stories that need to be told. He is merely a vehicle of a greater story of immorality and occupation and destruction, but also of an immeasurable patience, an unyielding *tawakkul*, and an indomitable defiance in the face of erasure.

I've waffled back and forth all day, wanting to delete the Instagram post that shows Mahmoud's carefree smile. *We shouldn't have done this*, I think. But it's too late; the train has left the station. Mohamad Abdelfattah and Adam Hamawy are on the *Ayman* show. Mohamad looks thinner than when I saw him last year.

It's a harrowing interview. Adam and Mohamad do an excellent job of keeping the interview focused on how dire the situation is in Gaza: a 1:7 ratio of ICU nurses to patients, pediatric patients dying every hour, burn victims slowly deteriorating from a lack of resources. Adam shares how what's happening in Gaza is worse than what he's seen in any combat zone in his twenty years as an Army surgeon: "I've done more amputations and seen more traumatic amputations on children in the last two weeks than during my entire career." He adds that he is only treating noncombatants.

It's the angle we had wanted them to take—to not be the focus of the story but to continue focusing attention on Gaza—but it's not a result of our reminders. It's simply who these men are. It is unnecessary to ask those who have already been selfless in action to then be selfless in their narrative. It is their instinct.

Day 15: Monday, May 13

It is Monday, the day that Mahmoud was supposed to have left Gaza. I call the airline to rebook his flight, but when they ask me what date to change it to, I have no answer, so I cancel it altogether.

The "test convoy" that was supposed to leave on Monday doesn't. Instead, a UN vehicle heading to European Hospital arrives riddled with bullet holes, its windshield cracked. The IDF shot two of the aid workers inside, despite the UN coordinating its movements with Israel and the UN insignia clearly marked all over the van. Mohamad receives one of the UN staff. She has a bullet injury to her neck that has fortunately bypassed all the major vessels and spared her nerves. The other person isn't as lucky—the IDF killed him.

The news makes headlines, but it's not quite as shocking as the World Central Kitchen killings. There are no consequences for Israel—what does it matter that they killed another aid worker? This one is Indian anyway, not British or Australian or Canadian—an obviously more palatable death.

The State Department spokesperson Vedant Patel recites so clearly and so embarrassingly off a script about how this is a "complex situation" and that the State Department is aware of the humanitarian issues related to it. And so Mahmoud, Mohamad, and everyone else there are reduced in this way to hand wringing and talking points, with no condemnation, no sense of urgency, and no promise to act.

My anxiety still rears its head here and there. Did the UN vehicle go to European Hospital to assess the situation because I sent that video of Monica with her IV to the media? Did we set in motion the events that would lead to one of them being killed? Had our media coverage put the target on their backs? Was the IDF trying to send a message by killing the UN aid worker?

I keep coming back to the belief that I have very little influence over what happens, even though in times of uncertainty the anxious instinct is to scramble for more control than one truly has over a situation. I continue to do my part by staying involved and sharing the truth while leaving the outcome to Allah—He is in control, not me. *Qaddara Allahu wa ma sha'a fa'al.*

Dina sends me a text asking me to verify some information: "Is this correct: 'I heard the doctor who saved Tammy Duckworth is among those stranded.'"

I pass it on to Mahmoud.

"Yes," Mahmoud replies. "He amputated her leg. Saved her arm. Nov 12, 2004." He continues: "Adam doesn't want it to be a big deal. He knows she wrote his name in her book. But he said he treated her like any other patient."

I respond to Dina. "Yeah, it is. Apparently, she wrote about it in her book."

An hour later, the news is tweeted: "Update: One of the American doctors trapped in Gaza by Israel's siege is Adam Hamawy,

an Army veteran who famously saved the life of @SenDuckworth
after her helicopter crash in Iraq."

I screenshot it and send it to Mahmoud.

"You can let him know the cat's out of the bag." It ends up
being seen over a million times.

Khidr and Abdelkarim receive a WhatsApp that Mahmoud is
stuck in Gaza, and they go down to visit him. It is a whole day
ordeal to find a taxi willing to drive down to European Hospital.
"We heard you were in trouble!" they tell Mahmoud, and he finds
it half comical and half shameful that his "plight" has reached
their ears—he has none compared to them. Still, Mahmoud is
happy for the excuse to see them.

Mahmoud brings out a bag of chocolate espresso beans, and
they smile—both at the taste and the memories. They sit together
and Abdelkarim enjoys the Nescafe in the doctors' dormitory; he
hasn't had any at all since the start of the siege. Mahmoud learns
that Khidr's sister was living in Rafah, and she is one of the ones
who evacuated ahead of the invasion. His brother's house has
also been destroyed, so now thirty people are living in one home.

When it comes time for them to leave, Mahmoud sifts through
his luggage to give them the resources he brought for them. He
gives them NICU supplies from his friend, a neonatologist who
went to Gaza after Mahmoud's first trip and found that al-Aqsa
Hospital's NICU was in desperate need. He also pulls out a few
bags of Crocs, but he sees that one of the pairs has two right
shoes.

"I don't know how I packed just the right shoes," he says sheepishly.

"*Malish*," Abdelkarim says.

"Wait a minute," Mahmoud thinks. "Why don't you give one each to someone who, um, only has a right foot?"

Abdelkarim shrugs. "That's actually not a bad idea."

Abdelkarim gives Mahmoud the *mamoul* his mother made for him, and he doesn't hesitate to take it; it is a nod to their friendship. After an hours-long wait for a donkey cart that can take them back up north, Mahmoud wishes them safe travels. He hopes to see Khidr and Abdelkarim again someday; it hurts a little more to say goodbye this time, without any idea of when he will leave Gaza or, if he does, when he will be able to return.

Abdelkarim tells Mahmoud, "If there's a ceasefire one day inshallah, you will come up and meet my mother, and she will feed you *maqlubeh*."

Mahmoud hopes so.

Day 16: Tuesday, May 14

The test convoy of UN staff has finally passed through the Kerem Abu Salem border crossing unscathed, with everyone still alive. I continue to be inundated with texts and emails, many from reporters asking to talk with Mahmoud or sometimes with me. My old coworkers message me. They saw Mahmoud on the news last night. The Montessori emails. They saw that Mahmoud is stuck and they want me to know they are here for me and Maymuna if we need anything.

Sarah's phone-banking campaign is ongoing, with so many volunteers that the representatives' assistants begin answering the phone with, "We know, you're the twentieth call about this today." I keep insisting that no one life has more value than any other, but I also see the momentum of the mobilizing going on for Mahmoud. I see that for many it's made what has been happening in Palestine for months more personal, and I also see that it exposes in me that I am mobilizing for Mahmoud as though his life does have more value.

I'm just getting off of a call when I see a message: "Ilhan Omar is waiting, are you still joining?" I completely forgot that someone had scheduled a meeting with the congresswoman that I am now ten minutes late to. I jump on the video call, just as I attended a meeting with some senator's aide earlier today. Representative Omar is gracious about my tardiness, and she asks me some questions about Mahmoud and voices her concerns about the situation in Gaza. I want to have faith in the process and trust that everyone is doing what they can, but I have little confidence in the political system as a whole anymore. These meetings with senators and congresspeople feel entirely useless—what will they say that hasn't already been said? Maybe they are less about me or Mahmoud and more about everyone else needing to feel like they're doing something too.

I say my piece, we end our meeting, and I put my trust in Allah. I go through my refrains:

Allahu akbar. God is greater.

Qaddara Allahu wa ma sha'a fa'al. Allah has decreed it and what He wills has happened.

Hasbi Allahu wa ni'mal wakil. Allah is sufficient for me and He is the best Disposer of Affairs.

"I think they will give me more than I give them," Mahmoud had said during his first trip to Gaza. It remains true. Perhaps not by choice, but the Palestinians' efforts to be free have revealed so many of our truths to ourselves: truths of selective morality, of the power of faith, and of the human capacity for hope.

Mahmoud's friend who was supposed to be on the mission entering Gaza yesterday is still waiting in Cairo. PAMA has not yet received word on whether this next mission will be allowed in or not. I ask Mahmoud if he had the option to leave, without knowing if PAMA or anyone else could come in, would he leave? He says he thinks he would. It would be difficult, but he believes it would be the right thing to do—his mission is technically over. What he is most afraid of is not the possibility of being unable to leave; it is the possibility of leaving and then, from the comfort of home, watching European Hospital in the news, empty and burned and decimated the way al-Shifa was.

He asks me what I think he should do. The truth is I don't know. I heard Mahmoud's interview on NPR yesterday, his description of the patients' fear of the foreign doctors leaving. How the doctors are in some sense a human shield for them, without whom they would be left vulnerable to slaughter by the Israelis. Is it more honorable to stay, or is it futile? The Israelis will do as they want, regardless of Mahmoud's presence. So does he have more of an obligation to evacuate when he can, and then return for a rebuild?

I call Maheen. I tell her of my guilt. She sounds withered when I ask what she thinks the right thing to do is. "All I know is this, Samaiya, when Maymuna was here on Sunday, she kept asking for her Baba. She really needs him home."

"Tomorrow is Wednesday," one of the many generous people helping with PR tells me over the phone. "We are going to start needing families in front of the media if we don't see any movement."

I hope she means someone else's family, because I refused to talk with Channel 8 when they just called and said they were on the way to our suburb, and I punted the NBC 5 interview to my sister Sarah, who has the emotional wherewithal to put herself together. I can barely change from pajamas to clothes.

She must be reading my mind because she goes on to say, "You'd be a sympathetic figure to have in front of a camera, with some coaching. A young mother, a doctor yourself." I cringe.

The PR world sometimes feels incredibly sleazy, slotting people here and there like chess pieces. Yet I've been participating in it myself, asking Mahmoud to make sure Monica joins him when he does the Fox 4 News interview because she is white and her name is Monica.

"What about Donya?" I ask. "Her name is easier to pronounce."

She ignores me completely. "Let's see about getting Monica's husband, too."

"Ok, but for now I have to go," I tell her.

Meanwhile, Dr. Hamarshi is interviewed on NPR's *Here & Now*, as a follow-up to Mahmoud's interview, to talk about PAMA's efforts to get their doctors out of Gaza and get their new doctors in. He talks about their coordination with the UN and the WHO. He talks about the WHO's attempts to negotiate with Israel for the next set of eleven doctors waiting in Cairo to get in, but there's still no update. He insists on the need for a cease-fire to be able to meaningfully help. Without it, the doctors are essentially putting a Band-Aid on a broken leg.

This isn't a normal conflict. It is madness. Even getting the doctors out is only a temporary measure. What is needed is a ceasefire, and even that is the bare minimum. What is needed is not just for the death to stop, but for the right to live to prevail: an end to the occupation.

Day 17: Wednesday, May 15

There's no update on Mahmoud's return, but I still try to go back to work on Wednesday.

On some conscious level, I realize the absurdity of trying to do my job while compartmentalizing whether the father of my children will be able to get out of a war zone. But on a more deep-seated, subconscious level, the mantras I have internalized for so long are not easy to fully let go of:

"My value is in my productivity."

"My worth is in my work."

"I matter if I achieve."

After I had Maymuna, I cut back to 50% in the psychiatric ER, to one and a half shifts instead of three. This meant I was away from Maymuna for fourteen hours straight only one day a week. I would walk to the pumping room four times during that shift. I would watch the nanny cameras and see Maymuna cry, and the nanny try her best to soothe. I would want to intervene, to call and tell her how it's done, but realized I needed to let them learn about each other too.

One of the first days after my return from maternity leave, I weighed a decision on whether to involuntarily hospitalize a patient. I had a whole discussion with the resident on the merits of hospitalizing versus discharging, and then signed the paperwork and gave it to the health unit coordinator. She came back to my desk a few minutes later and said, "Uh, Dr. Mushtaq? There is already an involuntary commitment for this patient from last night." It was inconsequential to the patient—it only meant that their transfer was already in motion—and the social worker and I had a bit of a chuckle about it, but I felt the shame of my intellectual horsepower having dwindled. The proverbial "mom brain."

Eventually, I left the psychiatric ER. I didn't want to miss Maymuna waking up and going to sleep in the same day. I switched to another service with more family-friendly hours, and worked mostly from home. I knew this was what I needed to do for myself as a mother, to make the transition into motherhood smoother for me. Yet whenever my own mother would call and ask, rather innocuously, "You're just at home today? You're not at the hospital?" I would feel the shame bubble back up. I wasn't a mother who was doing it all.

It took me years to understand that my career success was a vicarious dream I inherited as a daughter, but that it didn't have to be my own dream for myself as a mother, and I could give myself the space to separate the two.

Still, when I see my mother at the door, I'm not sure what to say. I haven't told her that I have taken off from work; I don't want to hear her surprise or her anxiety about the potential implications of doing so: "Will they fire you?" I don't have the emotional reserve to alleviate another set of anxieties about my job security when I'm barely managing my own about my partner.

Perhaps it is because she thinks I am working or because the situation is just so extraordinary, but whatever the reason, my mother continues to show up dutifully at my house each weekday afternoon between 3 p.m. and 5 p.m.—the middle shift between when Maymuna comes home from Montessori and my neighborhood's rotation starts. I stay holed up in my office doing the other work of . . . is it coordinating press? Joining political meetings?

Or simply worrying? I learn that one thing about crisis situations like this is that the rest of life doesn't get put on pause. The fan in my AC unit isn't working, so I have to find an HVAC guy. And the deadline to contest my property taxes is today.

Qasim is getting heavy and still cries more than Maymuna did, and it is difficult for my mother. Her fatigue is apparent, as is the toll Mahmoud's trip to Gaza is taking on her. I want to shield her from it, to take it on by myself, to not burden her with what she cannot bear. And so I don't ask her to continue coming or to stop coming. I let her do as she wishes, what she feels she should do. Maybe everyone who knows Mahmoud needs to feel like they are doing something, and so maybe that's why she says on her way out, "Don't worry, I will be here tomorrow too." And she is. She comes each day, as only a mother would.

Mahmoud wakes up this morning to the loudest sound he's ever heard. It turns out it was a bomb close by. He goes to the ICU to change the dressings on a patient he had cleaned up yesterday after a tracheostomy, and who had finally begun resembling the little boy that he is. He finds that he has passed away. The boy was the only survivor of his family, and Mahmoud thinks maybe it's better for him to be in Janna with them. He closes his eyelids. There is a *dua* to make specifically for this, for closing the eyes of the deceased, but he can't recall it, so he makes *dua* for the boy's soul.

European Hospital's administration asked the foreign doctors to provide some teaching for the local staff, and, despite the air strikes, a handful of nurses come from Nasser Hospital for it.

The thirst for knowledge he encounters in Palestine never fails to amaze Mahmoud. Even with infrastructure decimated and life constantly at risk, the Palestinians continue to memorize Quran or learn skills in health care, seeking knowledge truly until the grave. Mahmoud, Monica, Dr. Omar, and Suzanne, one of their Palestinian Jordanian colleagues, share some learning points on burn management, infectious disease, and caring for wounds. During Monica's section, another large bomb goes off near the hospital, shaking the building and causing her to lose her balance. Almost to her own surprise, she catches herself and immediately continues on with her lecture.

The World Central Kitchen intersects with Mahmoud's trip again, but in a much different way than it did the first time. This is where his meal for today comes from—bread with tomato paste, za'atar, and *labne*. He never in his life imagined requiring a meal from a volunteer kitchen.

The hope that has buoyed him thus far is starting to deflate some. What if there really is no plan for getting them out? The interview requests keep coming. Mahmoud works during the day, takes a small break for dinner, and then does the on-air interviews, but they feel repetitive and ineffective. I can see his sadness projected through the television screen.

Mohamad is no longer journaling, and Mahmoud has stopped writing his nightly reflection WhatsApp message. He is worried the media interviews have taken a toll on them, reducing their personal experience of Gaza to two-minute sound bites for people to watch over their gluttonous dinners before they move on to the next thing. His message is plain: stop the massacre. What else needs to be reported?

Mahmoud's op-ed will be published in the *Los Angeles Times* tomorrow. We go back and forth on the edits. "It's all about me," he says. "I want to include that I am gaining from their strength more than I am doing anything for them."

It feels like a message in a bottle put out into a sea of apathy, but he ends his essay saying the very least he can do is testify to the strength of the people of Gaza and convey that he is honored to be in their company.

Mahmoud sends me a picture from Maymuna's school, the back of her head as she faces forward in circle time. "I miss Maymuna's curls," he says. "I want to be honored by being with my family, too."

Even though I can't hear his voice, I know the pain he is feeling. "Mahmoud, continue your *dua* and recitation," I remind him. "Talk to Allah, not only the people. Maybe Allah will unseal their hearts through you. Trust in Him. Inshallah, you will be home in no time."

Day 18: Thursday, May 16

"I've been depressed," Mahmoud says. "I'm sleeping in longer. I'm not working as much." The patients aren't recovering; it feels like the hospital has become a hospice. They've run out of soap in the ICU. Looking for gloves feels like checking under couch cushions for spare change; people sift through drawers or the backpacks they came with to try and find a fresh pair, and if they can't find new ones, they reuse yesterday's gloves. The ICU mortality rate is nearing 100%, largely because of the spread of infection; if people survive trauma, they often die a slower death from diseases that would have been treatable outside of Gaza.

Mahmoud sends me a picture of a young Gazan boy smiling while cutting a watermelon. "When I saw the watermelon, I was so happy," he says. "Mohamad felt bad that we are eating it when others haven't had watermelon for months. How can one person be so happy and the other be sad?"

I know this feeling; I know the isolation of that abyss. I remember how happy Mahmoud was during those newborn days with Maymuna, and how sad I was, and how nonsensical the disparity between us seemed. I know he is holding out his hand the way I was back then, and I reach for it.

"Well," I start. "It's like you and me. When one is down, the other can help uplift."

Mahmoud says that while he was sleeping, Mohamad was in the ICU this morning doing CPR on a little girl. She died. "He said she had orange braids in her hair. Glitter on her fingernails. I wish I had been there with him. I think I'll go talk to him and help him feel better."

There are still no updates on when they will leave. No more convoys have left since the test convoy on Tuesday. I wonder what it is like for Mahmoud over there. He's confident they will leave eventually—likely soon, he tells me. The media attention is persistent. Adam Hamawy, who has been to multiple combat zones, remains unfazed—it's not his job to figure out his own exit. Most of the refugees have moved by this point to al-Mawasi, and much of the local staff has evacuated too. European Hospital has been reduced to foreign doctors treating women and children. There wouldn't be any basis for attacking the hospital. But there wasn't a basis at the other hospitals either. There can't ever be a basis for zip-tying babies in a hospital, killing patients and burying them in mass graves while they still have IV lines. Yet despite how catastrophic it sounds from here, Mahmoud remains hopeful, reassuring me in the face of an entirely uncertain and unprecedented situation.

I remember how uncertain things were at the start of our marriage too, in March of 2020.

One night after an urgent care shift, Mahmoud didn't look like his normal self. "We should probably talk about advanced directives, just in case." It was the gravity of how many people he'd tested for COVID that day, and the death rates his medical school friends in New York were seeing, that had shaken him. When he shaved the beard he'd had for almost twenty years so that his N95 would have a tighter seal, I barely recognized him.

Around the same time, I was designing mental health trainings for the company I was working with, where there was a strong focus on developing the skill of uncertainty tolerance.

That the more we could get used to living without knowing, being comfortable with our own ignorance about what the future holds, the more we could let go of our natural cognitive distortions to predict the future and anticipate the negative, and the more mentally healthy we could be. The pandemic had pulled back the veil on the uncertainty all of us were already living with; those who struggled the most were the ones trying to maintain the delusion that they had more certainty than they really did.

This is the principle I must embrace now. Uncertainty tolerance. And I am equipped to, because it was this that marked the difference between myself as mother to Maymuna and myself as mother to Qasim: Maymuna's arrival into my life split wide open my need for control, and in the crucible of early motherhood, I was made pliant, growing to accept my lack of certainty about even what I could achieve that day, yielding the idea that I had to achieve anything at all, trying to internalize the new core belief that my worth was not in my productivity. It was through the unpredictability of my young baby's whims that I learned to make peace with the vulnerability of parenting a child, of being in charge of someone so helpless—growing them, fashioning them, loving them with no expectation of anything in return, and no certainty whatsoever of who they will become when they grow up. Indeed, no certainty that they will even grow up at all. That vulnerability as a parent is what convinced me that there can be no certainty—not then, not now.

On the last day of his first mission to Gaza, before leaving European Hospital to go to the Rafah border, Mahmoud donated his blood. Unsure of when his last day will be this time, he makes his way to the hospital's transfusion center. There are so few patients, and so many of the ones they have are dying, so perhaps he can be of use this way.

When he arrives back at the dormitories, he sees that the team had been called into an urgent meeting while he was away. He walks in, and the PAMA lead tells Mahmoud that he is leaving tomorrow.

Their exit will not be through the way they came in. There won't be a UN convoy. They will have to get to the border on their own—and he's not sure to which crossing. Erez would mean crossing the whole strip. Kerem Abu Salem is closer, but it is usually reserved for trucks, not people.

Once they cross the border, the US embassy will be waiting on the other side to take them through Jerusalem. They will have to buy a plane ticket departing from Tel Aviv within twenty-four hours. But because the US embassy is transporting them to Tel Aviv, those with a green card who are permanent residents but not US citizens will not be allowed to exit—Israel will not issue them a visa.

That leaves eight of them within PAMA who would even be eligible to leave. Fewer than those who are not.

Adam Hamawy doesn't think twice. "I'm staying. Some American doctors have to stay to make sure everyone else gets out," he says. "We're all going to leave eventually," he reassures everyone on the team who isn't being evacuated. Dr. Omar, the trauma surgeon, is one of them—he is an American resident, but he has a Sudanese passport. He knows it's unlikely that the US embassy will go to bat for their permanent residents, but Adam reassures everyone who can't leave, "If some of us stay back, they're not going to abandon us."

He looks over to Mohamad sitting next to him, then at Mahmoud. "Take your chance. Some people have to go, and some people have to say," he says to them. He knows they have young kids. "You don't know when you'll get the chance again."

Mohamad and Mahmoud don't say much, but they nod at each other.

Monica, meanwhile, is crying and hugging Suzanne. Because she is Palestinian Jordanian, Suzanne can't leave even if she wanted to. Jomana, the team's neurologist, says she will pray *istikhara* and talk to her family about whether to leave or not, and Tamer, one of the nurses, decides to stay behind with Adam.

"So it's just five of us leaving," Mahmoud texts me.

Along with Suzanne, Dr. Omar, and the others who aren't being offered an exit, Jomana, Adam, and Tamer decide to stay behind.

As has often been the case with these messages, there are more questions than answers from me. Are you able to talk? When will you leave? Who's facilitating the exit? Is this public? How will you be safe en route?

Mahmoud knows few details. The car is a regular car—unmarked and driven by a Palestinian driver. He is worried about the transit; there is plenty of opportunity for the Israelis to drop a bomb on them. The IDF knowing their coordinates matters not in the least; they knew the coordinates of the World Central Kitchen convoy and struck it anyway. They knew those of the UN convoy that they shot at too. Both were marked. The Israeli army killed them, called it a mistake, and washed their hands of it. Just this week, Human Rights Watch released a report that Israel struck aid workers' known locations at least eight times in the last seven months, killing or injuring over thirty aid workers. The transit actually feels more dangerous than staying in the hospital, even with the air strikes' proximity to European Hospital.

"Just found out it will be through Kerem Abu Salem," Mahmoud writes. "We are less than ten minutes from the border. The driver will drive very fast."

I tell Amina about how slimy I feel that the evacuation is only for the Americans. Did we split the team by pushing for the State Department to get involved? I wonder. If we hadn't, would they all remain stuck?

Amina feels the complexity too. "But if Israel is determined to kill everyone, it is only symbolic to stay," she says. Amina is a filmmaker, a master at how the story is spun. She tells me all the narratives. "When the doctors kept saying, 'We won't leave unless the new doctors get to come in,' it read as 'OK, they don't want to leave.'"

I hadn't considered that, and I hadn't even read any of the comments on the news pieces.

"If you read comments, you'll see folks writing things like 'Well, it's their choice' and calling them 'Hamas sympathizers,'" she continues. "And if something happens to them, all America has to say is, 'We gave them the option to leave.'"

"Gosh. Brutal truth," I say.

She doesn't spare me. "Going to be really, really honest—they did not have enough white people to have the negotiating power they thought they had."

Amina isn't wrong. It's the painful reality of this world. Mahmoud is a Mahmoud, not a Michael. To the American layperson watching on Fox News, the P on their PAMA vests is a slur, and Mahmoud and Mohamad's names alone evoke images of Hamas fighters before they do volunteer doctors. Despite being American foreign aid workers while in Palestine, they would only ever be seen as foreign doctors in America.

This is the hierarchy of the West—not all lives have equal value. A Palestinian life is worth less than an Israeli life. Mahmoud's death is worth less than Monica's. Adam—an Arab, but with a name that can cross both cultures and an American military career—is probably somewhere in between. The fact that he saved Sen. Duckworth gives him a little more leverage—maybe not enough to get the next set of aid workers in, but enough to get the current group of doctors out, and I can't imagine that in the second he made his decision to stay, he hadn't already worked out that calculus.

Day 19: Friday, May 17

Mahmoud, Mohamad, Monica, and two other team members bid farewell to the local staff. One of Mohamad's colleagues in the ICU is in tears; it's an excruciating goodbye for them all. Their PAMA team sees them off outside the hospital. Even Mohamed Tawfik, who normally spends every potential minute working, has come for their departure. "*Bessalameh*," he tells them.

There are two cars for the five of them. Mohamad had joked that the safest seat is next to Monica, and he, Monica, and Mahmoud do end up in the same car; the trade-off, though, is that it is a worn-out Mercedes from the 1980s with a cracked windshield looking like it's on its last fumes. Picking which seat to take feels like playing Russian roulette. There's usually that one survivor if the car gets bombed, but there's no predicting which seat spares someone, if any. Mahmoud takes the front.

He looks at the map that the PAMA lead gives the driver. The route doesn't make sense. They are to zigzag through the rubble going north and make an upside-down U through Khan Younis before heading back south toward Rafah, then drive along the Philadelphi corridor to the Kerem Abu Salem crossing. This isn't going to be a twenty-minute straight shot, not at all. He is off by at least a few hours.

Mahmoud stares at the needle hovering over the *E*. The driver catches him looking. "Don't worry brother, it is broken." Mahmoud remains convinced the car will run out of gas in the middle of the drive.

The car moves at ten miles per hour weaving through Khan Younis, and Mahmoud is horrified by the sight of it. The sewage. The smell. The craters. The destruction. The complete disregard of basic principles. The hospital can sometimes be a bubble, almost a shield from the more massive destruction going on outside of it. It's the first time they've been out in Gaza in seventeen days, and what they see is that Khan Younis is essentially gone.

If the gas gauge is not broken, the AC certainly is. They can't keep the windows closed because it starts to become sweltering in the car, but when they open them, the flies start darting in and out. The driver maneuvers through the destroyed roads, stopping at certain points as if waiting for an imaginary green light. Once they reach the Philadelphi corridor, they wait for over an hour as shelling and gunfire continue two hundred yards away, plumes of smoke closer than they had ever seen them. The car ahead of them resumes, and they try too—but the car won't start.

The other NGO's van and the first PAMA car keep going, and they start to look smaller as the distance between their car and the rest of the convoy widens. Mohamad starts to feel uneasy; their car already looks like a local car, and now it has fallen behind the pack—not moving despite the instruction to. An Apache helicopter had been hovering over their heads not too long ago. He knows what they look like to the Israelis: a target.

"It's out of gas, isn't it?" Mahmoud asks the driver.

"No, no!" he says, waving his hand. "It just needs a push."

Well, Mahmoud thinks, this is one way to go. He says his *shahada* to himself and then to Mohamad he says, "*Shid halek*,"—literally, strengthen yourself—and they get out of the car quickly, Mahmoud pushing from the passenger side and Mohamad from the driver's side. They push until the driver pops the clutch and the engine starts, and they jump back in to catch up to the rest of the convoy.

They are passing along the Rafah border crossing, but Mahmoud doesn't recognize it at all. Pictures taken there, prayers made there—it's all barren land now. Even the green oasis, the smallest slice of life and beauty, has been destroyed. He only knows it is Rafah because of the bulldozers clearing the rubble from the homes they saw being bombed on their arrival more than two weeks ago. Mohamad catches sight of the sign they saw when they entered: *Ahlan wa sahlan bi Falasteen.* Welcome to Palestine. This time, though, there is an Israeli soldier with an M16 on either side of it—as if saying, like Mahmoud had dreamed, "Welcome to Israel."

They have to stop again, and another hour passes. They set out again slowly, making their way toward Kerem Abu Salem. Mohamad sees the opening in the concrete wall, their passage out of Gaza. But as the convoy nears it, an Israeli tank comes speeding out of nowhere, blocking their exit, and turns its gun right on them.

"Watch," Mohamad says, "they're going to have this gun in our face for an hour."

"If it's past an hour, you know I'm getting right up there and talking to them myself," Monica says—perhaps she has picked up enough Arabic to have understood Mahmoud saying "*Shid halek*." Mahmoud knows, though, that it's one thing to step out and push the car and another to get in the face of a tank. It's a power play by the IDF—a show of force. He opens his window, puts his vest over his head to keep the flies out, and waits.

My eyes pop open. Despite keeping the lights on, I accidentally nodded off. When I last heard from Mahmoud, they were driving through a decimated Khan Younis.

I instinctively reach for my phone and squint to make out the bright red numbers of the digital clock on my dresser: 3:44. Mahmoud last messaged at 2:59. "We've been just waiting at the border for about an hour. In our car with flies all over the place. So much so that a fly went straight inside my mouth." He tells me about how the sun is beating down on them and says, "This is what the West Bank Palestinians go through every single day, waiting at these checkpoints."

"Mahmoud, how are you?" I ask, hoping to catch him in real time.

"Waiting by a concrete wall," he tells me. They are still at the border on the Palestinian side, still within sight of the bombs and the smoke and the shelling. "I hate this place. I wish I stayed," he writes.

He doesn't tell me that they had been staring at the barrel of a tank gun for over an hour, that the tank accelerated toward them, trying to intimidate them, before finally moving out of their way. I won't learn that part until much later. He also doesn't tell me about the Israeli bedouins who man the crossing, how they are the ones he wants to interact with the least, that they are talking to him in Arabic, as if they have something in common.

The bedouin looks at Mahmoud's passport and waves him through.

"We crossed," Mahmoud messages me.

I can hardly believe it. I feel like I've been stuck myself, waiting for this decrescendo, hoping to find out that Mahmoud is safe, and yet so very distraught over the circumstances of his leaving. I feel terrible for the position he was put in.

I call Mahmoud's sister in California. I know she has been sleeping with one eye open too. She picks up almost immediately, despite it being the middle of the night.

"Mahmoud's out," I say softly, as it starts to sink in more for me too. The week of uncertainty—of not knowing when, not knowing how, not even knowing if—is really over.

I can hear her breathe a heavy sigh. "Alhamdulillah. Alhamdulillah," she whispers into the phone. "Thank you so much for telling me."

I pray two rak'as of Salat al-Shukr, a prayer of thankfulness. I close my eyes. All I feel is gratitude. I'm not sure if I nod off or I blink before I hear Qasim waking up, crying for his early morning feeding.

On one side of the Kerem Abu Salem crossing is Gaza, still under siege, and on the other side is a US embassy caravan awaiting the health-care workers who have left, including the five from PAMA. At least a dozen plain white vans and cars outfitted with bulletproof windshields, with no flags or insignia, are lined up one behind another. The doors open simultaneously, and several buff white men, armed and donning bulletproof vests and black sunglasses, step out of the cars. It looks like a scene out of a hostage rescue movie.

"Welcome home," one of the men calls to the group.

Home. Safety. For them, for the ones who got out, but not for the Palestinians whose homes have been invaded.

"Where's Maa-mood?" another man with a gun strapped to his waist asks.

Mahmoud raises his hand slightly. "Here."

"I'm Jerry," the man says, holding his hand out. Mahmoud shakes it. "You're the PAMA lead?" he asks.

"Well, just for this transport," Mahmoud says.

"It's great to see you guys," Jerry says. "We've been waiting for you since seven this morning. Now we know this can be done—all it took was a phone call from Biden."

A phone call. That was it. That is what it took to get Mahmoud and the others out. That is what it could take to end the entire thing too.

Mohamad, the bolder of the two, tells Jerry, "We had a tank pointing a gun at us for an hour."

Jerry shakes his head, his concern apparent. "Yes, that incident reached us."

The Israeli soldiers at the border start yelling at them, gesturing for them to get in the cars and get out.

Mohamad looks over at the soldiers, then back at Jerry. "How do you like being here?" he asks facetiously.

Jerry looks right at him. "I completely hate it. Those guys," he says, pointing at the Israeli soldiers, "disrespect us so much. Never had as many guns pointed at us as we do here."

Mohamad keeps asking for more details as the five of them pile into the car, and Jerry keeps sharing. "These guys told us not to go to the West Bank, to stay away from the Palestinians, they'll throw rocks at you. It's the complete opposite," he says. "We feel so welcome when we go to Jerusalem. Still prefer a burger over a shawarma though."

"They're like that just with you guys?" Mohamad asks.

"Everyone. From the staff to the whole administration," Jerry says. "Disrespect, all the way up. Even to Blinken."

"Why do you guys put up with it? We're the ones arming them. What's Biden's strategy here?"

"You want my honest opinion? We have no idea what the administration is doing. The situation in Gaza is terrible."

Mahmoud wonders if maybe Jerry is as opposed to the genocide as he is.

"Do you guys go to the border often?" Mohamad asks.

"Well, we were here October 8 to pick up hostages," Jerry says. "We waited all day, and then we were told to return."

Mohamad keeps pressing. "Who told you that?"

"Higher-ups," Jerry replies. "No hostage deal."

"Take Me Home, Country Roads," starts playing, a song that Mohamad heard nonstop during his fellowship training in West Virginia. He can't help but tear up. There's also an instant sense of being back in America, from the car's cool leather seats and air conditioning to the plentiful store of water bottles. It doesn't feel like they deserve all this safety when nothing has changed for the people in Gaza.

It's a change of pace for Mahmoud too to be back among Americans and a strange dichotomy as well; he left one home on a convoy through Gaza, and feels right at home here too in this

American convoy. If he were in Mr. Armstrong's class today, he would again refuse to stand for the flag in protest of the genocide in Gaza, and perhaps twenty years ago that could have been considered anti-American. But today Mahmoud is certain that he is both American and a witness for Palestine.

Monica asks what each of them is feeling, and it is complex and layered: guilt at leaving; a sense of pride in their government for working to get them out; sadness at the destruction; relief—sweet relief—to be going home.

Just before Maymuna turned one, Mahmoud used the last of his paternity leave for the three of us to visit his extended family in Jordan. When we shared that we were planning to go to the West Bank to spend a few days in Jerusalem, they were shocked. Despite living only about one hundred kilometers away, most of them had never been; they would have to jump through multiple hoops as Jordanian citizens, if they would even be allowed entry at all.

We have a favorite photo from that first day in Jerusalem of Maymuna in her pale-blue dress giggling with Mahmoud, his head tilted back and lines around his eyes from laughing so hard, the gold of the Dome of the Rock glinting in the background. We were so happy we could go to the mosque with her, see her first tooth come in there in its courtyard, show her the site of the Prophet Muhammad's ﷺ ascension, where I happened to see an adjoining plaque that bore her namesake: "Maymunah asked Prophet Muhammad ﷺ: 'O Messenger of Allah! Tell us about Jerusalem.' He said: 'Jerusalem is the Land of the Gathering and

Resurrection. Go there and pray in it, for one prayer in it is the equivalent of a thousand prayers in other places.' Maymunah asked: 'What if I could not reach it?' He said: 'Then you can send a gift of oil to light its lanterns, for he who does this it is as if he has traveled to it.'"

Maymuna was blessed to reach Jerusalem before her first birthday, and now reaching al-Aqsa Mosque and being in that sanctuary again a year and a half later is the only real balm for Mahmoud. He FaceTimes me from there in the courtyard of the mosque, and I see his face live for the first time in over two weeks. I see the beautiful turquoise architecture and the gold dome glinting in the background, just as it did in the photo of him with Maymuna a year and a half ago. He is twenty pounds lighter, and he smiles at me through his tears.

Day 20: Saturday, May 18

Mahmoud and Mohamad get haircuts in Jerusalem to clean up before reuniting with their families. Mahmoud knows how much I don't like his screen-print T-shirts, so Mohamad gives him one of his nicer ones to wear on the flight home. They walk around Jerusalem for hours, eating sandwiches, exploring the old city, praying inside al-Aqsa Mosque. They drink water without rationing it. Mahmoud hears from the drivers who took them to the border—they made it home at 9:30 p.m., waiting for hours at the border for the green light to leave after dropping off the PAMA team.

Without Mohamad sleeping by him as he has for the last few weeks, and with the massive sleep debt he's accumulated, Mahmoud sleeps right through the Fajr *adhan*. Mohamad, however, goes back to the mosque to pray.

An IDF soldier stops him.

"Where are you from?" he barks at Mohamad.

"America," Mohamad replies.

The soldier doesn't accept it. "Where are you really from?" he asks louder.

Mohamad isn't afraid. Looking squarely at the Israeli soldier, he says, "My family is from Nablus."

The IDF soldier knows that Palestinians from Nablus can't make it here to Jerusalem, even though they are both in the West Bank. "So how are you here?" he asks Mohamad.

"I'm a doctor. I was providing aid in Gaza."

The soldier sneers at him. "Get away from here then, and go back to Gaza."

Mahmoud prays Dhuhr at al-Aqsa Mosque and then leaves for the airport. His flight is a few hours before Mohamad's, and it's the first time he is away from him in three weeks. There is an emptiness being on his own; he feels a longing to be with everyone again. He wonders if they made a mistake by leaving, if they should have waited until they could all leave together.

On the way to the airport, Mahmoud is stopped at the first checkpoint. He learns that the vast majority of Arabs are—even Israeli ones—while Israeli Jews are allowed to go straight through. The car undergoes a full search at the separate lot that Arabs are sent to. Everything is searched—the trunk, the hood, the undercarriage.

Mahmoud and the driver are allowed to pass through after the search. The driver remarks at how the airport has been largely empty since October 7; there are more workers than travelers. They stop at an ATM so Mahmoud can pay him in shekels, and then Mahmoud finds his way to the security point for non-Jews, where an advanced screening is conducted, much longer and more invasive than the secondary screening in the US. His bags are screened and he sees the guards stop at the most outlandish things—examining his trimmer for five minutes and weighing his bag of za'atar, then telling him he has to dump it because it is over twenty grams.

At the gate, waiting to board his flight out of Tel Aviv, Mahmoud is thinking about all the *shuhada* who have already passed and all the injured who will pass too, and all the suffering he has borne witness to in these past few months. He thinks about the hadith Modhir had mentioned, about the angel of death coming for Musa (*alayhi al-salam*). Musa (*alayhi al-salam*) resisted, then let death overtake him. He was at the end of his prophetic mission, and he returned to Allah for his reward. He imagines the reward of the *shuhada*; he imagines the children reunited with their parents, who will remember no suffering after only a dip in Janna. This life truly is not everything, and perhaps the wisest are those ready to let it go.

Day 21: Sunday, May 19

Mahmoud should be arriving late morning today, a weekend, so I should have plenty of time to get the kids ready, park at the airport, and wait for him inside. Sarah, her husband, and a few of Mahmoud's friends are planning to be at the airport to welcome him home too.

I think back to finding out he was coming home early Friday. Shortly after, I attended the closed State Department meeting for families. They briefly discussed the evacuation, but there was little expressed in the way of comfort to the families or appreciation for the aid workers, and much reference to the State Department Travel Advisory, as if the group had gone in as blundering tourists rather than humanitarians.

That evening, I went to a dinner where both Representative Ilhan Omar and Shaykha Haifaa Younis, a practicing OBGYN who herself went to Gaza, were also in attendance. Dr. Haifaa was in the same group as Omar, Mahmoud's brother, volunteering at al-Aqsa Hospital shortly after Mahmoud left his first mission. She talked with us about what she saw there—stories of a young boy, fearless in front of an Israeli tank, memories of how every single person she met there recited the Quran with such beauty, and lessons that we can learn from the Palestinians about life and faith.

I introduced myself to her after the dinner as Mahmoud's wife. She embraced me; she had heard Mahmoud was in Gaza and stuck there after the Rafah invasion. I told her that he was in Jerusalem now.

"You were OK with him going to Gaza?" she asked.

"I was," I replied. "I accepted that what is meant for him will find him, here or there."

Dr. Haifaa smiled and held my shoulders. "You are a courageous woman."

I smiled back. I don't know if I am. She is the woman who has gone to Gaza. And there are countless women who remain in Gaza by choice.

Yet I wonder about what Mahmoud's friend said to me before he left the first time. That I would be on that plane too if it weren't for the kids. That in this phase of my life, my reward in staying—my acceptance of motherhood—is equivalent to that of Mahmoud's in going.

I wonder if it is in fact courage that I've had in other points in my life. Sometimes courage has meant leaving and sometimes it has meant diving in. Perhaps it is courage simply to make a choice—whichever choice—when it is difficult to make. Trying again, going for it a second time, knowing the risks. Taking that leap and having faith.

I told Shaykha Haifaa about how Mahmoud was left with the choice to leave or stay, and what Shaykh Omar Suleiman said when I asked him—that there was not a sinful choice, but there was a more noble one. I asked her what she thought Mahmoud should have done. She told me that she would have prayed *istikhara* and followed the result, and I told her what Mahmoud had said, that he was going to the border and leaving the result with Allah.

"If one leaves it to Allah, then it is He who decides best," she said. "Don't let Shaytan convince you otherwise."

On the way home, I called Donya. It felt so different talking to her from this place of shared relief, knowing our Babas were coming home to their young children, yet also sadness at the lack of any more doctors going in. We also shared worry for those left behind, including Adam Hamawy who, in choosing to stay with the rest of his team to ensure that they could get out too, would be missing his daughter's graduation ceremony this weekend.

I wonder if there is a before-and-after moment in life where it gets easier to let go. Does it become a different calculus when the kids are grown? What was the demarcating line in the life of Dr. Shamisa, after which he could say, "it would be an honor," or after which Dr. Hamawy became the kind of person who stays behind, knowing the risks? I wonder if it ever gets easier to let go of the ox hairs—or rather, to never reach for them in the first place—and to accept death whenever it comes, the way Prophet Musa (*alayhi al-salam*) did even though he was still a distance from the Holy Land. Letting go, taking the leap of faith, accepting that the end has come now.

Mahmoud sleeps almost the whole flight back. Only one checkpoint is left between him and his family, and it is on American soil.

"Where were you?" the border control agent asks him.

"Gaza," Mahmoud replies.

"Oh, my," the agent says. It's not a location he hears routinely, certainly not in the last year, and it's a change of pace from the summer vacation destinations of the other travelers who arrive via connections through Dubai. "What . . . what were you doing there in Gaza?"

"I volunteered as a wound care doctor," Mahmoud answers.

"Hmm." He looks at his employer information, his medical ID badge. It's good enough for him. He stamps Mahmoud's passport and lets him pass.

Mahmoud almost misses the entourage of friends who have come to the airport to greet him; he doesn't even notice the photographer from the local newspaper. His eyes land first on Maymuna, who is sitting on her bottom on the airport floor engrossed in a book, her pale little legs sticking out beneath her dress.

Mahmoud rushes to her and gets on his knee beside her. Maymuna turns away from her book to look up at him, stoic. She says nothing at all, the sadness apparent in her eyes, staring at him as if to say, "Baba, where have you been this whole time?" and guilt washes over Mahmoud as he takes her hand to kiss it.

I was where I needed to be, he thinks, and now I'm here where I belong.

How does one tell a story that has no end? Mahmoud returned safely from Gaza, but Gaza has not yet been delivered from Israel. Khidr and Abdelkarim, and countless others we do not know in life nor in death, remain. I wonder who the *shuhada* were in their lifetimes, and I wonder what will become of those who are still alive today.

All of life carries the unknowns of the weeks Mahmoud was in Gaza, and the unknowns of how long Gaza will be under siege. It's only when we look behind the veil of false certainty that we can view the depth of the unknowns we live with daily. We carry no true certainty; we only imagine we do. Gaza has removed that veil for me, perhaps permanently. It has strengthened my resolve in faith, because I don't know that any of us will ever witness justice for the Palestinians on this side. It has humbled me in front of my Lord, stripped me of complacency and sensitized me, yet again, to His greatness over everything.

The consequences of losing our humility are immense. We demand from life. We insist upon life. We feel entitled to life. We forget that all of life is a gift and an opportunity; we become heedless. Our complacency is so complete as to have rendered us unable to contemplate where we all go from here.

Perhaps the end is simply this: That even if we may strike death away in our homes when they are invaded, in the seas when the waves crash over us, in the lands when the bombs fall near us, that in some other time and in some other place, the only true certainty is that death will eventually find us, even in the loftiest of towers. And when it does, a lasting justice will be rendered, and glad tidings given to those who were patient.

Afterword

After the Rafah invasion, missions to Gaza were stopped. When they were allowed to resume, it was with new strictures: no Palestinian doctors, no medical supplies, and only four-week-long missions. The Kerem Abu Salem crossing was arbitrarily—and frequently—closed due to "security reasons" or because it was "only open Thursdays and Tuesdays."

In October, an essay in *The New York Times*[**] shared the testimony of sixty-five medical professionals who spoke out about the number of children they saw shot in the head while on medical missions in Gaza. Mahmoud, Mohamad, Monica, Adam, and Thaer were all mentioned. Despite the fact that the editorial included head scans of the gunshots, it elicited so much pushback that the paper published a rare statement insisting that the essay was "rigorously edited," adding that they did in fact corroborate and view actual images of the children shot in the head. They didn't include them because they were "too horrific for publication."

Only days after the essay was published, Israel denied entry to all medical missions that were authorized by the WHO, including PAMA and several others with which the participants in the essay had volunteered. It was difficult not to see the action as retributive.

[**] Feroze Sidhwa, "65 Doctors, Nurses and Paramedics: What We Saw in Gaza."

Six months had passed since Mahmoud was evacuated from Gaza, and the destruction continued unabated. Maymuna turned three, and forty-five Palestinians were killed that day. Qasim turned one, and sixty-two were killed that day. In the video Mahmoud filmed during his exit from Gaza, I remembered seeing the rubble on both sides of the track that his car drove through, and I often wondered what was left to destroy.

In November, Mahmoud heard about a team traveling to Gaza that was looking for a wound care doctor. I knew he would go again eventually; I had just hoped there would be a ceasefire by then. Yet here was the call to go again, and there wasn't one. But the months had changed me. Gaza had changed me. There was little in the way of discussion between us, no ambivalence to work through. He was ready to go, and I was ready to stay.

Mahmoud's departure was set for January 23, 2025. A few days before leaving, he received a voice note from Khidr in Gaza of cheers in the streets: a six-week ceasefire had been agreed to.

Agreed to—not enacted. In a psychologically brutal move, the cessation of fire was agreed to on Friday but scheduled for Sunday, and Israel continued to bomb Gaza for the next two days, killing over a hundred more Palestinians, some even minutes before the ceasefire's start time.

As the mission date drew closer, I wondered about how this visit would be different because of the ceasefire. I imagined Mahmoud treating emotional wounds in addition to physical ones, listening to the stories of the patients and what they had lost. He received a dinner invitation from Abdelkarim, and he marveled at their hope for the future. But it wasn't to be.

In Amman on the night before their team was slated to enter Gaza, Mahmoud and three others learned that Israel had denied their permit. They wouldn't be going.

Acknowledgments

Writing for me has often been about processing, and at the beginning of Mahmoud's first trip to Gaza, I wrote to work through my feelings about his mission. However, particularly in the aftermath of Mahmoud's second mission, I felt the need to write not only for myself, but to preserve a historical record of the events that transpired during his two missions in Gaza.

I didn't know where writing this story would lead, but once it became a book, I hesitated to publish it with my perspective in it. I worried that a memoir that included my viewpoint alongside Mahmoud's time in Gaza might be perceived as me centering myself amid a genocide. Yet I can only write what I know, and so I moved forward with this book as a testimony from a Pakistani American Muslim mother, who, like many others in America, has grappled with the tension of living a life of gross privilege and complicity while bearing witness to genocide from a remove, wishing desperately to be able to stop it.

I have only admiration for all the health-care workers who went to Gaza and have since shared their testimony with the world, and I appreciate those who shared their time and their experiences with me: Dr. Mahmoud Sabha, who spent countless hours with me excavating his stories and examining them with utmost scrutiny, and his colleagues Dr. Omar, Dr. Adam Hamawy, Dr. Mohamed Abdelfattah, Dr. Thaer Ahmad, and Monica Johnson. Thank you as well to Dr. Majdi Hamarshi and PAMA for their leadership in an unprecedented situation and for their enthusiasm for this book. To Donya, who was alongside me the whole way, just as our husbands were. To everyone who called their congressperson and senators, and everyone who kept us in their thoughts and their *duas*. Thank you feels like it falls short.

In sharing my perspective, I have also put words to the labor of women, which is often invisible. But it is the labor of women that enabled many physicians from across the world to go to Gaza—and of course, there were the women physicians, pharmacists, and nurses who were direct volunteers there on the front lines. It was largely the efforts of women that facilitated my own journey while Mahmoud was in Gaza, and for whom I must express my appreciation: the women who created the phone-banking campaign (Sarah and Yumna), the women who provided media support and legal input (Dina, Yasmin, Zeena, Nadia, Tahera, Lubna, Fatima, Maria, Tasneem, Mahdis, Hena, and Hebah), the wives of the other physicians who went (thank you for bringing us together, Naiema), and the women who brought meals or who helped me with my young children (Nasreen, Ashley, Ayesha, Samina, Sunna, Saamia, Barira, Safiya, Vendula, Shaista, Sumrah, Shandraya, Samrina, Aisha, Nazia, Khyrria, Merusha, Marium, Sarah U, Somir, Maheen, my mother, and my mother-in-law).

It was women who supported me with guidance along this publishing journey—Saadia Mian, Uzma Jalaluddin, Lilly Gharamenieh, Susan Golomb—and it was my dear friend Fatima who was my first reader (after my husband). Finally, it was women who brought this book to life—I have tremendous gratitude for the team at Daybreak Press: my editor Jessica Hassan, Fatema Hakim, Anse Najiyah Maxfield, and Dr. Tamara Gray.

This book explores themes of patience, sacrifice, and duty, both at home and in Palestine. Yet it is also very much a love story: the love between a wife and a husband, the love of a parent for their child, the love the indigenous have for their land, and the love a Muslim has for their fellow Muslim and for Allah. Love—if we let it—can be limitless, expansive, and inspiring. I must express my love here for my husband and my children, who are the essence of my life, and without whom neither this book nor anything in it would be possible.

Glossary

ﷺ: Arabic script for *salla Allahu alayhi wa sallam*. This phrase is used by Muslims after mentioning the Prophet's ﷺ name as a way of showing respect. It means "peace and blessings be upon him [the Prophet Muhammad]."

adhan: The Muslim call to prayer.

akhira: The next life, or hereafter.

al-Aqsa Mosque: The mosque in Jerusalem in the compound of the Dome of the Rock.

alayhi al-salam: An Arabic phrase meaning "peace be upon him," used to show respect after mentioning the name of a prophet.

Ahlan wa sahlan: A colloquial expression meaning "welcome."

alhamdulillah: "Praise be to God," a phrase used as an expression of thankfulness.

Allahu akbar: "God is greater," a phrase used in the call to prayer as well as an expression of faith.

al-Masjid al-Haram: The Great Mosque in Mecca.

amana: Trust.

Asr: The afternoon prayer.

batil: Variously defined as null, false, of no value.

Bessalameh: "With peace," a colloquial expression meaning "Godspeed."

dada: Urdu word for paternal grandfather.

Dhuhr: The noon prayer.

dua: Supplication, invoking God or asking from Him.

dunya: This world or life, as opposed to the hereafter.

Eid: One of the two major Islamic holidays.

Eid al-Fitr: The first day of the month of Shawwal, the Muslim holiday that celebrates the end of Ramadan, the month of fasting.

Fajr: The dawn prayer.

fi sabilillah: "In the cause of God."

hadith: The sayings, actions, and silent approvals of the Prophet Muhammad ﷺ, which form a major source of guidance for Muslims together with the Quran.

Hajj: The Muslim pilgrimage to Mecca.

hasbi Allahu wa ni'mal wakil: "Sufficient for *me* is God and He is the best Disposer of Affairs."

hasbun Allahu wa ni'mal wakil: "Sufficient for *us* is God and He is the best Disposer of Affairs."

hifdh: Memorization (often of the entire Quran).

hijab: Headscarf.

hudna: Ceasefire.

huffadh: People who have memorized the entire Quran.

iftar: The meal to break one's fast at sunset.

imam: A Muslim leader of prayer or a Muslim leader of a mosque.

inshallah: "God willing"; a phrase expressing hopefulness about an event in the future.

Intifada: Uprising.

Isha: The night prayer.

israf: Excess.

istikhara: A *dua* (invocation) and salah (ritual prayer) for seeking specific guidance from God for a decision.

janaza: Funeral.

Janna: Heaven.

Jannat al-Mu'alla: A cemetery in Mecca near al-Masjid al-Haram.

Jiddo: Grandfather.

jihad: Struggle, referring to the inner spiritual struggle against the lower self or struggle against enemy forces.

jilbab: An overcoat, often worn by women when going outside or to the mosque.

Jumua: Friday, or the Friday congregational prayer.

khatira: A short spiritual speech or reminder.

khimar: A long headscarf that covers the arms.

labne: A thick yogurt served as a dip; common in the Levant.

La hawla wa la quwwata illa billah: "There is no might nor power except with God"; often used as an expression when faced with difficulty.

Laylat al-Qadr: The holiest night in Islam; worship done on this night has multiplied rewards.

malish: A colloquial expression meaning "It's OK" or "No problem."

mamoul: Butter cookies, usually with date filling.

Maghrib: The evening prayer.

Maqam Mahmoud: "Praiseworthy Station," referring to the elevated status of the Prophet Muhammad ﷺ.

maqlubeh: "Upside down"; a traditional Palestinian dish of rice, meat, and vegetables that is ceremonially turned upside down from its pot onto a serving platter.

m'sakhan: A traditional Palestinian dish of chicken, red onions, and sumac.

mujahideen: Muslims who engage in jihad as it relates to armed struggle.

munafiq: A hypocrite.

murabitun: Muslims who keep watch (ribat) at the frontier of the community as a means of protection and defense.

murajaʿah: Revision undertaken by those who have completed the memorization of the Quran.

Nakba: Literally "the catastrophe"; the event in which the borders of Israel were drawn and thousands of Palestinians were expelled from their homeland.

nikkah: Marriage ceremony.

qadr: Destiny, or divine decree.

Qaddara Allahu wa ma shaʾa faʾal: "God has decreed, and whatever He wills, He does."

qari: A reciter of the Quran.

Quran: The primary Islamic text believed to be divine revelation and the literal word of God.

rakʿa: A unit of salah (prayer) comprising specific movements and invocations.

Ramadan: The month in which Muslims fast.

rizq: Provision.

ruku: Bowing to God.

sabr: Patience, steadfastness.

salah: Ritual prayer; in Islam, there are five daily ritual prayers at specific times of the day and night (Fajr, Dhuhr, Asr, Maghrib, and Isha).

Salat al-Janaza: Ritual funeral prayer.

Salat al-Shukr: Ritual prayer of gratitude.

shahada: The testimony of faith in Islam. It is "I bear witness that there is no God but Allah, and Muhammad is the Messenger of God."

shahid: Martyr.

sharia: Islamic law.

Shawwal: The month after Ramadan, in which it is recommended to follow up Ramadan with six fasts.

shaykh/shaykha: A male/female Muslim scholar.

Shaytan: Satan.

shid halek: An Arabic phrase meaning, "gather yourself" or "strengthen yourself."

shuhada: Plural of *shahid*; multiple martyrs.

suhur: The meal before starting a fast at dawn.

sujud: Prostrating to God with one's head on the ground.

Tafaddal: A colloquial expression meaning "Here you go" or "Go ahead."

tarawih: Night prayers offered only in the month of Ramadan.

tawakkul: The Islamic concept of reliance upon God.

Teta: Grandmother.

ummah: The global Muslim body.

wajib: Obligatory.

wudu: The ritual purification Muslims make before praying.

yaqeen: Certainty; the Islamic concept of complete conviction in God.

za'atar: A spice blend of dried herbs common in Arab countries.

About the Author

Dr. Samaiya Mushtaq is a psychiatrist, mental health educator, and writer. Samaiya earned her medical degree from Vanderbilt University prior to completing a four-year residency in psychiatry. As a physician, Samaiya's career has spanned academic psychiatry, consulting, and health-care administration, with an interest in mental health in Muslim communities. Samaiya's essays and editorials have been published in *The New York Times*, in *The Dallas Morning News*, and on Muslimmatters.org. She resides in Dallas, Texas, with her husband and children. Outside of work and spending time with family, Samaiya can be found cooking, writing, or completing a crossword at a local coffee shop.